W9-CBD-701

Friendship
GIFTS
OF GOOD TASTE

*T*hroughout our lives, we reach out and tie our
hearts to others, creating friendships that bring us
continual joy and comfort. Thoughtful words and
actions that express our love and appreciation help
us nurture these bonds. Looking back, though, I
remember times along the way when I wish I had
been better at telling my friends how much I cared.

This book is for all of us who sometimes need a
little help putting our feelings into words. Using the
book is simple; just choose the quotation that reflects
your feelings, and there's the perfect gift to convey
your love. Whether it's a batch of cookies or a
charmingly decorated cake, when you give a friend
what you make with your hands, you're giving the
greatest gift of all — your heart.

Anne Childs

LEISURE ARTS, INC.
Little Rock, Arkansas

Friendship GIFTS OF GOOD TASTE

EDITORIAL STAFF

Editor: Anne Van Wagner Childs
Executive Director: Sandra Graham Case
Creative Art Director: Gloria Bearden
Executive Editor: Susan Frantz Wiles

PRODUCTION
Managing Editor: Sherry Taylor O'Connor
Foods Editor: Susan Warren Reeves, R.D.
Crafts Designer: Patricia Wallenfang Sowers
Senior Technical Writer: Kathy R. Bradley
Technical Writer: Dawn R. Kelliher
Production Assistants: Diana Heien Suttle and
  Nancy L. Taylor
Test Kitchen Assistant: Nora Faye Womack

EDITORIAL
Associate Editor: Dorothy Latimer Johnson
Senior Editorial Writer: Linda L. Trimble
Editorial Writer: Laurie R. Burleson
Editorial Assistants: Marjorie Lacy Bishop and
  Barbara Cameron Ford
Advertising and Direct Mail Senior Copywriter:
  Eva M. Sargent

ART
Production Art Director: Melinda Stout
Senior Production Artist: Linda Lovette
Art Production Assistant: Cindy A. Zimmerebner-Johnson
Photography Stylist: Karen Smart Hall
Typesetters: Cindy Lumpkin and Stephanie Cordero
Advertising and Direct Mail Artists: Sondra Daniel and
  Kathleen Murphy

BUSINESS STAFF

Publisher: Steve Patterson
Controller: Tom Siebenmorgen
Retail Sales Director: Richard Tignor
Retail Marketing Director: Pam Stebbins
Retail Customer Services Director: Margaret Sweetin
Marketing Manager: Russ Barnett

Executive Director of Marketing and Circulation:
  Guy A. Crossley
Fulfillment Manager: Scott Sharpe
Print Production: Nancy Reddick Lister and
  Laura Lockhart

MEMORIES IN THE MAKING SERIES

Copyright© 1991 by Leisure Arts, 5701 Ranch Drive, Little Rock, Arkansas 72212. All rights reserved. No part of this book may be reproduced in any form or by any means without the prior written permission of the publisher, except for brief quotations in reviews appearing in magazines or newspapers. We have made every effort to ensure that these recipes and instructions are accurate and complete. We cannot, however, be responsible for human error, typographical mistakes, or variations in individual work. Printed in the United States of America. First Printing.

International Standard Book Number 0-942237-14-5

Table of Contents

Table of Contents

Table of Contents

If you need to say "I goofed" — for missing a friend's birthday, forgetting a lunch date, or for any reason — here's a lighthearted way to make amends! Chock-full of candy-coated chocolate pieces, our delicious No-Fail Microwave Fudge is quick and easy to make. A Shaker box gaily decorated with polka dots and comics makes a whimsical carrier for the candy.

NO-FAIL MICROWAVE FUDGE

3½ cups confectioners sugar
½ cup cocoa
¼ teaspoon salt
½ cup butter or margarine, cut into pieces
¼ cup milk
1 tablespoon vanilla extract
1 cup candy-coated chocolate pieces

In a large microwave-safe bowl, combine first 3 ingredients; stir until well blended. Drop butter into sugar mixture. Microwave on High 1 to 2 minutes or until butter melts. Add milk, stirring until smooth. Microwave on High 1 minute longer. Stir in vanilla and chocolate pieces. Pour into a buttered 8-inch square baking pan. Chill 1 hour or until firm. Cut into 1-inch squares. Store in an airtight container.

Yield: about 5 dozen squares fudge

COMICS BOX

You will need a Shaker box; flat black spray paint; white paint pen; comics; clear lightweight vinyl (available at fabric stores); red grosgrain ribbon same width as side of box lid; craft glue; waxed paper; and white paper, tracing paper, and a black felt-tip pen for tag.

1. Spray paint box and lid black; allow to dry. Use paint pen to paint dots on side of box; allow to dry.
2. Use a pencil to draw around lid on vinyl and on wrong side of comics. Cut out circles ½" larger than drawn lines.

At ½" intervals, clip comics and vinyl to ⅛" from drawn lines.
3. Center comics circle right side up on lid. Pulling paper taut, glue clipped edges to side of lid; allow to dry. Repeat for vinyl circle.
4. Cut ribbon ½" longer than lid circumference. Glue ribbon to side of lid, covering edges of comics and vinyl.
5. Line box with waxed paper and fill with fudge.
6. For tag, trace balloon pattern onto tracing paper; cut out. Use pattern and cut tag from paper. Write "OH FUDGE!" on tag and draw outline around edge.

6

A friend who enjoys gardening will love this little crate filled with surprises! The tangy Radish Jelly is an unusual treat that's delicious with meat or cream cheese and crackers. To accompany the decorated jar of jelly, stencil radishes on a pair of canvas work gloves and include a trowel and packets of seeds — everything your friend will need to grow a new crop of radishes.

RADISH JELLY

  2 cups (about two 6-ounce bags)
         finely chopped radishes
2½ cups granulated sugar
 ¾ cup water
  1 box (1¾ ounces) pectin
  2 teaspoons prepared horseradish

In a large stockpot, combine first 3 ingredients over medium-high heat; stir constantly until sugar dissolves. Bring to a rolling boil. Add pectin; stir until dissolved. Bring to a rolling boil again and boil 1 minute longer. Remove from heat; skim off foam. Stir in horseradish. Following Sealing Jars instructions, page 120, pour into jars. Store in refrigerator. Serve with cream cheese and crackers or meat. Include serving suggestions with gift.

Yield: about 2 pints jelly

RADISH CRATE

You will need a wooden crate, 1 pair of light-colored canvas garden gloves, tracing paper, graphite transfer paper, tagboard (manila folder), craft knife, cutting mat or a thick layer of newspapers, removable tape (optional), stencil brushes, paper towels, green and red fabric paint, black permanent felt-tip pen with fine point, fabric for jar lid insert, craft batting, lightweight cardboard, craft glue, paper for tag, hole punch, green felt-tip pen, 3-ply jute, green excelsior, radish seed packages, and a trowel.

1. For gloves, use radish pattern and follow How to Stencil, page 122, to stencil radish design on gloves. Use black pen to draw roots on radishes.
2. Follow paint manufacturer's instructions to heat-set designs if necessary.
3. For jar lid insert, follow Jar Lid Finishing, page 122.
4. For tag, cut tag shape from paper. Punch hole in pointed end. Use green pen to write ''Radish Jelly'' on tag. Tie jute around jar lid, thread ends of jute through hole in tag, and tie ends into a bow.
5. Fill crate with excelsior. Place trowel, jar of jelly, seed packages, and gloves in crate.

Come and share a pot of tea, my home is warm and my friendship's free.

As aromatic and delicate as the flower itself, Rose Petal Tea makes a charming gift for a friend who adores old-fashioned things. This wonderful blend is reminiscent of the Victorian era when blossoms from the garden were a popular ingredient in salads, sandwiches, and desserts. As a graceful gesture, present the tea mix in a dainty basket topped with a sentimental cross-stitched lid.

ROSE PETAL TEA

2 cups firmly packed fragrant rose petals from pesticide-free blossoms (about 15 large roses), washed and patted dry

1 cup tea leaves

Preheat oven to 200 degrees. Place rose petals on an ungreased baking sheet. Leaving oven door slightly open, dry petals in oven 3 to 4 hours or until completely dry, stirring occasionally. In a food processor fitted with a steel blade, process rose petals and tea leaves until finely chopped. Store in an airtight container. Give with instructions for brewing tea.

To brew tea, place 1 teaspoon tea for each 8 ounces of water in a warm teapot. Bring water to a rolling boil and pour over tea. Steep tea 5 minutes, stir, and strain. Serve hot or chilled.

Yield: about 3 cups tea

TEA BASKET

You will need a rectangular basket with an opening at least 8¾" x 6⅝" (we used a basket with an 8¾" x 6⅝" opening), a piece of Cream Lugana (25 ct) 3" larger on all sides than opening of basket, fabric for lining (see Step 3 for amount), a 2"w bias strip of fabric and 3/16" dia. cotton cord for cording and 1½"w pregathered lace trim (see Step 4 for amounts), 1⅓ yds of ¼"w grosgrain ribbon, thread to match Lugana and cording fabric, medium weight fusible interfacing, craft batting, medium weight cardboard, embroidery floss (see color key, page 10), embroidery hoop (optional), and craft glue.

1. Work design, page 10, on Lugana using 3 strands of floss for Cross Stitch and 1 for Backstitch and Half Cross Stitch.
2. Cut a piece of interfacing slightly smaller than stitched piece. Follow manufacturer's instructions to fuse interfacing to wrong side of stitched piece.
3. Measure basket opening. Cut 1 piece from cardboard and 2 pieces from batting same size as basket opening. With design centered, trim stitched piece to ⅝" larger on all sides than basket opening. Cut lining fabric same size as stitched piece.
4. Measure circumference of basket opening; add 2" to measurement. Cut lace trim, bias strip, and cord the determined measurement.
5. For cording, lay cord along center on wrong side of bias strip. Matching long edges, fold strip over cord. Use a zipper foot and machine baste along length of strip close to cord. Matching raw edges and starting 1" from end of cording, baste cording to right side of stitched

piece; clip seam allowance as needed. Open ends of cording and cut cord to fit exactly. Insert 1 end of cording fabric in the other; fold raw edge of top fabric ½" to wrong side and baste in place.
6. With right sides facing and matching straight edge of lace trim to raw edge of stitched piece, baste lace to stitched piece, overlapping ends ½"; trim excess.
7. For ties, cut ribbon in half. Fold each length in half. Referring to Fig. 1 and matching fold of ribbon to raw edge of stitched piece, pin 1 ribbon to center top edge on right side of stitched piece; repeat for bottom edge.

Fig. 1

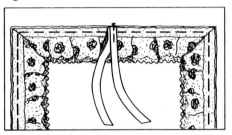

8. Place stitched piece and lining fabric right sides together. Being careful not to catch ribbon ends in stitching, use a zipper foot and sew pieces together along 3 edges, sewing as close as possible to cording. Clip corners diagonally and trim seam allowance; turn right side out and press.
9. Glue both pieces of batting to 1 side of cardboard.
10. With batting side of cardboard facing wrong side of stitched piece, insert cardboard into open edge between stitched piece and lining. Sew final closure by hand. Remove any visible basting threads.
11. Place a plastic bag of tea mix in basket. Place lid on basket. Thread 1 end of each tie through basket rim and tie into a bow. Trim ribbon ends.

Continued on page 10

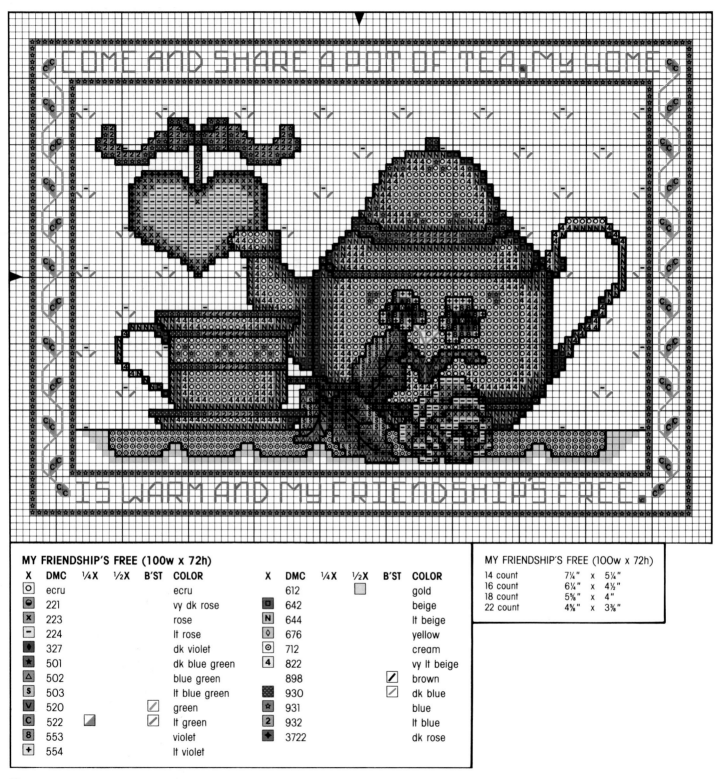

MY FRIENDSHIP'S FREE (100w x 72h)

X	DMC	¼X	½X	B'ST	COLOR		X	DMC	¼X	½X	B'ST	COLOR
○	ecru				ecru			612			■	gold
◐	221				vy dk rose		■	642				beige
X	223				rose		N	644				lt beige
-	224				lt rose		◇	676				yellow
◆	327				dk violet		⊙	712				cream
★	501				dk blue green		4	822				vy lt beige
△	502				blue green			898			╱	brown
S	503				lt blue green			930			╱	dk blue
V	520		╱		green		✿	931				blue
C	522	◢	╱		lt green		2	932				lt blue
8	553				violet		◆	3722				dk rose
+	554				lt violet							

MY FRIENDSHIP'S FREE (100w x 72h)

14 count	7¼"	x	5¼"
16 count	6¼"	x	4½"
18 count	5⅝"	x	4"
22 count	4⅝"	x	3⅜"

Friendship makes the rough road smooth.

This luscious Rocky Road Tart is a great remembrance for anyone who makes your journey through life a little smoother. Topped with toasted marshmallows that look like tiny cobblestones, the dessert features a chocolate-almond crust and a gooey chocolate filling. For a creative presentation, cover your pie box with a map and tag it with a cute "highway sign."

ROCKY ROAD TART

CRUST
- 1 cup granulated sugar
- 1 cup all-purpose flour
- 1 cup finely ground almonds
- 1 teaspoon baking powder
- ½ cup butter or margarine
- 2 ounces unsweetened chocolate
- 1 teaspoon vanilla extract

FILLING
- 6 ounces (two 3-ounce packages) cream cheese, softened
- ½ cup granulated sugar
- ¼ cup butter or margarine, softened
- 2 tablespoons all-purpose flour
- 1 egg
- ½ teaspoon vanilla extract
- ½ cup slivered almonds
- 1 cup (6 ounces) semisweet chocolate chips
- 2 cups miniature marshmallows

Preheat oven to 350 degrees. For crust, combine first 4 ingredients in a medium bowl. In a small saucepan, melt butter and chocolate over low heat, stirring until smooth. Add chocolate mixture and vanilla to dry ingredients; stir until dough is crumbly. Press evenly into bottom of a greased and floured 9-inch springform pan.

For filling, beat cream cheese, sugar, and butter in a medium bowl until fluffy. Beat in next 3 ingredients. Fold in almonds and chocolate chips. Spoon batter evenly over crust. Bake 40 to 45 minutes or until a toothpick inserted in center comes out clean. Spread marshmallows evenly over top. Bake 4 to 5 minutes longer or until marshmallows are light brown. Cool in pan 10 minutes. Remove sides of pan; cool completely. Store in an airtight container.

Yield: 8 to 10 servings

For box, spray a road map lightly with Design Master® glossy wood tone spray; allow to dry. Follow Gift Box 2 instructions, page 123, to cover box with map. We covered a 9″ pie box and decorated it with 1¼″ wide paper ribbon and ¼″ wide jute braid trim. *For tag,* trace pattern onto tracing paper; cut out. Use pattern and cut tag shape from paper. Use a black felt-tip pen to write "Rocky Road Tart" on tag and to draw a line ⅛″ from edge.

Friends are the sunshine of life.
—JOHN HAY

Like sunshine to flowers, friends help us flourish and bloom. Our wildflower basket of sweet, creamy Orange Curd is the perfect way to say thank you to such an encouraging companion. Touched with the goodness of sun-kissed fruit, the delicate spread is a delicious accompaniment to cookies or hot breads. The sunny arrangement of flowers will be a lasting reminder of your special friendship!

ORANGE CURD

  1 cup milk
  1 cup whipping cream
  ½ cup frozen orange juice
      concentrate, thawed
  1 vanilla bean, cut in half
      lengthwise
  6 egg yolks
  ⅔ cup granulated sugar
  1 tablespoon all-purpose flour

In a large saucepan, combine first 4 ingredients over medium heat. Bring to a boil; remove from heat. Cover and let stand 15 minutes. Remove vanilla bean and use a sharp knife to scrape black seeds from bean into milk mixture. Return bean to milk mixture.

In a medium bowl, whisk remaining ingredients together until smooth. Add ½ cup milk mixture to egg mixture; stir until well blended. Add egg mixture to remaining milk mixture in saucepan.

Stirring constantly, cook over medium-low heat 7 to 10 minutes or until mixture coats the back of a spoon. Do not boil. Remove from heat; strain mixture. Store in an airtight container in refrigerator. Serve with cookies, muffins, or toast. Include serving suggestions with gift.

Yield: about 2½ cups orange curd

WILDFLOWER BASKET

You will need an approx. 9″ dia. grapevine wreath; artificial berries, wildflowers, leaves, and grass; medium weight cardboard; a 2″ x 2″ x 4″ block of floral foam; sheet moss; an artificial butterfly; hot glue gun; and glue sticks.

1. For basket bottom, cut a circle of cardboard to cover wreath opening; glue to back of wreath.
2. Glue floral foam into 1 side of basket.
3. Line basket with a layer of sheet moss, covering foam; glue to secure.
4. Arrange berries, flowers, leaves, and grass in floral foam and along 1 side of basket; glue to secure. Insert small pieces of moss around berries, flowers, leaves, and grass and between vines of basket.
5. Place a jar of orange curd in basket. Glue butterfly to lid.

"Mint" to be friends.

A bottle of our creamy Mint Cordial can help you tell someone special that you were meant to be friends. Thick and frothy, the beverage has a cool, refreshing flavor. To accompany the cordial, we tucked a pair of liqueur glasses and a box of mints in a decorated basket. The handwritten tag is prettily accented with a tiny nosegay of dried flowers matching those on the basket.

MINT CORDIAL

  1 can (14 ounces) sweetened condensed milk
1½ cups whipping cream
  1 cup peppermint schnapps
  2 teaspoons vanilla extract

Pour all ingredients into a blender and blend until smooth. Store in an airtight container in refrigerator. Shake well before serving. Serve chilled.

Yield: about 4 cups liqueur

A batch of star-spangled cookies is sure to boost the morale of a loved one in the military who's based far from home. The sweet Honey-Almond Cookies are cut in heart and star shapes and decorated with red, white, and blue icing. For a special delivery, trim your cookie box in patriotic colors, too!

Preheat oven to 350 degrees. On a lightly floured surface, use a floured rolling pin to roll out dough to ¼-inch thickness. For patterns, follow Transferring Patterns, page 122. Place patterns on dough and use a sharp knife to cut out an equal number of heart-shaped and star-shaped cookies. Transfer to a greased baking sheet. Bake 10 to 12 minutes or until light brown. Transfer to a wire rack to cool completely.

For icing, combine sugar and milk in a large bowl; beat until smooth. Transfer ¾ cup icing to a small bowl; tint blue and cover. Transfer ½ cup white icing to another small bowl; add water and stir until smooth. Tint red and cover. Cover remaining icing. Ice star-shaped cookies blue and heart-shaped cookies white. Allow icing to harden. Use a small round paintbrush and red icing to paint wavy lines on heart-shaped cookies. Allow icing to harden. Store in an airtight container.

Yield: about 7 dozen cookies

HONEY-ALMOND COOKIES

COOKIES
- 1 cup butter or margarine, softened
- ⅓ cup butter-flavored shortening
- ⅓ cup vegetable oil
- 2 cups granulated sugar
- 2 eggs
- ⅓ cup honey
- 1 teaspoon almond extract
- 1 cup quick-cooking rolled oats
- 4 cups all-purpose flour

ICING
- 7 cups confectioners sugar
- ½ cup plus 2 tablespoons plus 2 teaspoons milk
- Blue and red paste food coloring
- 1 tablespoon water

For cookies, cream butter, shortening, oil, and sugar in a large bowl until fluffy. Add eggs, honey, and almond extract; beat until smooth. Add oats and flour; knead until a soft dough forms. Cover and refrigerate 1 hour.

Sharing is caring with a friend.

An intimate conversation shared over a cup of tea is sure to be enhanced by these delicious Praline Tea Cakes. Rich and moist, the maple-flavored cakes feature a buttery topping of brown sugar and pecans. A pretty covered mug tucked in your gift basket makes a nice accompaniment to the cakes.

PRALINE TEA CAKES

CAKES
- 1 cup butter or margarine, softened
- 1 cup granulated sugar
- 6 eggs
- 1 teaspoon maple-flavored extract
- 1 cup finely crushed vanilla wafer cookies
- 1 teaspoon baking powder
- ½ teaspoon salt
- ½ teaspoon dried grated orange peel

TOPPING
- 2 cups chopped pecans
- 1 cup butter or margarine
- 1 cup firmly packed brown sugar

Preheat oven to 350 degrees. For cakes, cream butter and sugar in a large bowl until fluffy. Add eggs and maple extract; beat until smooth. Add remaining ingredients; stir until well blended. Pour batter evenly into 12 greased and floured shortcake tins. Bake 15 to 20 minutes or until a toothpick inserted in center comes out clean. Cool in pan 10 minutes; invert onto a wire rack to cool completely.

For topping, preheat oven to 350 degrees. Spread pecans evenly on an ungreased baking sheet and bake 10 to 15 minutes, stirring occasionally. Remove from oven. In a medium saucepan, combine butter and sugar over medium heat. Stirring constantly, bring to a boil and cook 2 to 3 minutes or until mixture thickens. Stir in pecans. Spoon about 2 tablespoons topping into center of each cake. Allow to cool completely. Store in an airtight container.

Yield: 1 dozen cakes

New-made friendships, like new wine, Age will mellow and refine.

— JOSEPH PARRY

New friendships carry the promise of many good times to come. A bottle of sweet Blueberry Wine is a delightful way to celebrate such pleasant expectations. The delicious beverage is easy to make by adding fruit and sugar to white wine. To surprise a new friend, tuck the bottle into a pretty bag along with a ribbon-tied stack of matching napkins. A pair of elegant glasses to toast your friendship completes the gift.

BLUEBERRY WINE

   1 bottle (720 ml) dry white wine
   3 cups unsweetened frozen
         blueberries, thawed
  ¼ cup granulated sugar

Combine all ingredients in a large bowl; stir until sugar dissolves. Cover and chill 3 days to allow flavors to blend. Store in an airtight container in refrigerator. Serve chilled.

Yield: about 4 cups wine

Here's to good friends, good times, good health, good cheer.

This festive basket will make any gathering of friends a special celebration! A chilled pitcher of Wine Punch is included, along with cups, plates, and napkins. To add to the fun, we trimmed the basket with bright curling ribbon and tucked in lots of colorful party favors.

WINE PUNCH

  2 bottles (720 ml each) dry white wine
  2 cans (12 ounces each) frozen pineapple juice concentrate, thawed
  1 can (6 ounces) frozen lemonade concentrate, thawed
  1 can (6 ounces) frozen orange juice concentrate, thawed
  1 jar (10 ounces) maraschino cherries

In a 1-gallon container, combine first 4 ingredients, stirring until well blended. Stir in cherries. Cover and chill 8 hours or overnight to allow flavors to blend. Serve chilled.

Yield: about 3 quarts punch

A sporty friend who's into biking, biking, or any activity on the run will enjoy this Trail Mix. Loaded with nuts, raisins, granola, and pretzels, the energy-packed mix is easy to carry along — and it's perfect for snacking whenever traffic hazards or other obstacles call for a rest stop! A brightly striped bag with an eye-catching tag is a cute way to deliver your gift.

TRAIL MIX

½ cup dry-roasted peanuts
½ cup whole almonds
½ cup raisins
½ cup granola cereal
½ cup stick pretzels
1 can (14 ounces) sweetened
    condensed milk

Preheat oven to 300 degrees. In a large bowl, combine first 5 ingredients. Pour condensed milk over; toss until mixture is well coated. Transfer to a greased 9 x 13-inch baking pan. Bake 25 to 30 minutes, stirring occasionally. Transfer to aluminum foil to cool completely. Break into pieces. Store in an airtight container in refrigerator.

Yield: about 4 cups trail mix

For bag, use a 6" x 24" piece of fabric and follow Steps 2 - 4 of Fabric Bag instructions, page 122. Place a plastic bag of trail mix in bag. Tie a shoestring into a bow around bag. For tag, cut a 3" square from red paper; cut corners from square to form an octagon. Use ⅛" wide white vinyl tape to form white line on tag. Use ¾" high white vinyl press-on letters to spell ''STOP'' on tag. Use a black felt-tip pen to write ''TRAIL MIX INSIDE'' on tag.

When someone is ailing in body or spirit, a friend's smiling face is often ''just what the doctor ordered.'' You'll be the best cure ever when you deliver Chicken-Onion Soup in our chicken roost basket. Dijon mustard gives this old home remedy a zesty new flavor that's sure to encourage a speedy recovery.

CHICKEN-ONION SOUP

 4 tablespoons butter or margarine
 2 tablespoons olive oil
 5 medium onions, coarsely chopped
 4 cloves garlic, minced
 3 tablespoons all-purpose flour
 1 tablespoon Dijon-style mustard
 1 teaspoon granulated sugar
 1 teaspoon salt
 1 teaspoon ground black pepper
 ½ teaspoon ground thyme
 6 cans (14½ ounces each) beef broth
1½ cups dry white wine
 3 cans (5 ounces each) chicken, drained
 ⅓ cup cognac

In a large stockpot, heat butter and oil over medium-high heat. Add onions and garlic; sauté until tender. Add next 6 ingredients; stir until well blended.

Gradually stir in beef broth and wine. Stir in chicken. Bring to a boil; reduce heat to low and simmer 30 minutes. Remove from heat. Stir in cognac. Store in an airtight container in refrigerator. Give with serving instructions.

To serve, transfer soup to a large stockpot. Cook over medium heat 15 to 20 minutes or until heated through, stirring occasionally.

Yield: about 12 servings

For basket, fill basket with pieces of raffia; hot glue a small artificial chicken to basket rim. For label on jar, use pinking shears to cut desired size circle from cream-colored paper. Use a black felt-tip pen to write ''CHICKEN-ONION SOUP'' on circle. Use craft glue to glue label to a piece of wrapping paper. Use regular scissors to trim wrapping paper to ½" larger than label. Use craft glue to glue label to jar.

You're my sweetie pie.

The special man in your life will be glad he's your "sweetie pie" when you surprise him with this luscious tart! Topped with fresh sliced berries, our Strawberry Pie features a creamy filling nestled in a flaky pastry shell. A heart-shaped tag is a cute way to express your sentiments.

STRAWBERRY PIE

CRUST
    1½ cups all-purpose flour
     ½ teaspoon salt
     ½ cup vegetable shortening
     ¼ cup cold water

FILLING
    1 box (3 ounces) strawberry-
        flavored gelatin
    1 cup water
     ½ cup whipping cream
    1 package (8 ounces) cream cheese,
        softened
    1 cup confectioners sugar
    1 pint strawberries, capped and
        sliced

GLAZE
    1 teaspoon cornstarch
    1 teaspoon water
    3 tablespoons apple jelly
        Red food coloring

Preheat oven to 450 degrees. For crust, sift together flour and salt in a medium bowl. Using a pastry blender or 2 knives, cut in shortening until mixture resembles a coarse meal. Sprinkle water over; mix until a soft dough forms. On a lightly floured surface, use a floured rolling pin to roll out dough to ⅛-inch thickness. Transfer to a 9-inch pie pan and use a sharp knife to trim edges of dough. Prick crust with a fork. Bake 12 to 15 minutes or until light brown. Cool completely on a wire rack.

For filling, combine gelatin and water in a medium saucepan over medium heat, stirring until gelatin dissolves. Remove from heat; allow to cool to room temperature. In a chilled medium bowl, whip cream until stiff peaks form. In a large bowl, beat cream cheese and sugar until fluffy. Fold whipped cream into cream cheese mixture. Fold in gelatin. Spoon filling evenly into cooled crust. Cover and refrigerate until pie is set in center. Arrange strawberries over filling.

For glaze, combine cornstarch and water in a small bowl to form a paste. In a small saucepan, melt jelly over medium heat. Whisk cornstarch mixture into jelly; remove from heat. Stir in 1 or 2 drops food coloring. Brush glaze evenly over strawberries. Cover and refrigerate until ready to present.

Yield: 8 to 10 servings

Show a favorite teenager you think she's "the cat's pajamas" with this cute and comfortable ensemble. Sending along a batch of our Crunchy Cat Cookies, "dressed" in icing pajamas, is a charming way to complete the gift. Cornmeal and ground almonds give the shortbread cookies a deliciously different flavor. Whether she's hosting a slumber party for friends or enjoying a quiet evening to herself, she'll love wearing these "purr-fect" pj's!

CRUNCHY CAT COOKIES

COOKIES

1 cup butter or margarine, softened
⅓ cup butter-flavored shortening
⅓ cup vegetable oil
2 cups granulated sugar
2 eggs
1 teaspoon vanilla extract
3 cups all-purpose flour
1 cup cornmeal
½ teaspoon salt
1 cup finely ground almonds

ICING

1½ cups confectioners sugar
2 tablespoons plus 2 teaspoons milk
Purchased blue, pink, and white decorating icing
Black paste food coloring

Preheat oven to 350 degrees. For cookies, cream butter, shortening, oil, and sugar in a large bowl until fluffy. Add eggs and vanilla; beat until smooth. In another large bowl, sift together next 3 ingredients. Add dry ingredients and almonds to creamed mixture; knead until a soft dough forms.

On a lightly floured surface, use a floured rolling pin to roll out dough to ¼-inch thickness. For cookie pattern, use small cat pattern and follow Transferring Patterns, page 122. Place pattern on dough and use a sharp knife to cut out cookies. Transfer to a greased baking sheet. Bake 12 to 15 minutes or until light brown. Transfer to a wire rack to cool completely.

For icing, combine sugar and milk in a small bowl; beat until smooth. Spread icing on cookies to resemble pajamas. Allow icing to harden. For details on pajamas, use a small round tip to pipe blue and pink decorating icing on cookies.

Transfer white decorating icing to a small bowl; tint black. Transfer black icing to a pastry bag fitted with a very small round tip. Pipe icing on cookies to resemble eyes, nose, and whiskers. Allow icing to harden. Store in an airtight container.

Yield: about 6 dozen cookies

CAT'S PAJAMAS

You will need cotton-blend T-shirt pajamas; an 8½" x 11" sheet of acetate (available at art supply stores); craft knife; cutting mat or a thick layer of newspapers; removable tape (optional); stencil brushes; paper towels; cardboard T-shirt form; white and lt tan fabric paint; pink, blue, and black dimensional fabric paint in squeeze bottles; and black permanent felt-tip pen with fine point.

1. Wash, dry, and press pajamas. Insert T-shirt form into shirt.
2. Cut two 5½" x 8½" pieces from acetate. For cat stencil, use felt-tip pen to trace outline of large cat pattern onto 1 acetate piece. For pajamas stencil, trace outline of pajamas (blue area of pattern) onto remaining acetate piece. For placement guidelines, trace outline of cat using dashed lines. Use craft knife to cut out stencils along solid lines only.
3. Follow Step 2 of How To Stencil, page 122, to stencil 3 lt tan cats (1 upside down) on pajama top. Matching guidelines on pajamas stencil to outline of each cat, stencil white pajamas on each cat.
4. Follow paint manufacturer's instructions to heat-set cat designs if necessary.
5. Use felt-tip pen to draw eyes, nose, and whiskers on each cat.
6. (*Note:* Allow to dry after each paint color.) Use blue and pink paint to paint details on pajamas. Use black paint to write the following above the cats: You're "the cat's pajamas"!
7. Follow paint manufacturer's instructions to wash pajamas.

LARGE CAT

23

The only way to have a friend is to be one.

— RALPH WALDO EMERSON

A friend who needs a helping hand will welcome a gift of wholesome Chicken Paprika. The meaty rice casserole will provide a nutritious meal for the whole family with a minimum of effort. We discovered an adorable "chicken" basket to present our dish in, but any attractive carrier will be a lasting reminder of your thoughtfulness.

CHICKEN PAPRIKA

½ cup butter or margarine
1 medium onion, chopped
½ cup chopped celery
1 teaspoon dried minced garlic
2 teaspoons paprika
1 teaspoon salt
½ teaspoon ground black pepper
2 cans (5 ounces each) chicken, drained
½ cup all-purpose flour
1 can (10½ ounces) chicken broth
1 cup half and half
2 cups cooked rice

In a large stockpot, melt butter over medium heat. Add next 3 ingredients and sauté until onion and celery are tender. Stir in next 4 ingredients. Sprinkle flour evenly over chicken mixture; stir until well blended. Cook until heated through. Stirring constantly, gradually add chicken broth and cook until mixture begins to thicken. Stir in half and half and rice. Cook 5 to 10 minutes or until heated through. Remove from heat. Transfer to a 2-quart casserole. Cover and refrigerate until ready to present. Give with serving instructions.

To serve, preheat oven to 350 degrees. Bake covered 25 to 30 minutes or until heated through.

Yield: 6 to 8 servings

You're the cream in my coffee.

A good friend makes simple pleasures even more enjoyable. Sharing a jar of Chocolate-Malt Coffee Creamer is a fun way to let a friend know that she's a special ingredient in your life. Stirred into a cup of coffee, the mix adds creamy chocolate flavor spiced with a hint of cinnamon. For a country presentation, fill an old-fashioned milk bottle with the mix and tuck it into a pail adorned with a spotted bow and a small copper cowbell.

CHOCOLATE-MALT COFFEE CREAMER

- 2 cups instant hot cocoa mix
- ⅔ cup nondairy powdered coffee creamer
- ⅔ cup malted milk mix
- ½ teaspoon ground cinnamon

Combine all ingredients in a large bowl; stir until well blended. Store in an airtight container. Give with serving instructions.

To serve, stir 2 heaping teaspoonfuls into 8 ounces hot coffee.

Yield: about 3 cups creamer

COW PAIL

You will need a 1-gallon metal pail, 1½ yds of 1⅜"w black and white printed craft ribbon, florist wire, a 1¼"w copper cow bell, and straw.

1. Form a triple-loop bow from ribbon; wrap center of bow with wire to secure. Wire bell to center of bow. Wire bow to handle of pail.
2. Fill pail with straw. Place bottle of creamer in pail.

$\mathcal{T}$he best thing to give to a friend is your heart.

— FRANCIS MAITLAND BALFOUR

A basket of Chicken Pies is a tasty way to express your heartfelt appreciation to a friend. Cut in a heart shape, the flaky little pies are filled with tender chicken and vegetables. To make your gift extra special, include a set of appliquéd place mats. Our no-sew appliqué technique makes it easy to add country hearts to purchased mats; the "stitches" are drawn on with a pen.

CHICKEN PIES

FILLING

    1 cup frozen hash brown potatoes
    1 cup (about ½ pound) finely
        chopped uncooked chicken
    1 large onion, finely chopped
    ¼ cup grated carrot
    ¼ cup finely chopped turnip
    2 teaspoons garlic powder
    ½ teaspoon salt
    ½ teaspoon ground black pepper

PASTRY

    4 cups all-purpose flour
    1 tablespoon salt
    1 cup butter-flavored shortening
    1 cup ice water
    ½ cup butter or margarine, melted

For filling, combine all ingredients in a large bowl; stir until well blended. Cover and refrigerate until ready to use.

Preheat oven to 375 degrees. For pastry, sift together flour and salt in a large bowl. Using a pastry blender or 2 knives, cut shortening into flour mixture until mixture resembles coarse meal. Slowly add water, mixing until a soft dough forms. Turn dough onto a lightly floured surface and use a floured rolling pin to roll out dough to ¼-inch thickness. Use a 3-inch heart-shaped cookie cutter to cut out an even number of heart shapes. Transfer ½ of heart shapes to a greased baking sheet; spoon about 2 tablespoons filling on top of each heart shape. Place remaining heart shapes over filling. To seal, crimp edges with a fork. Brush tops with melted butter. Bake 45 to 50 minutes or until golden brown. Transfer to a wire rack to cool completely. Store in an airtight container in refrigerator. Give with serving instructions.

To serve, preheat oven to 350 degrees. Bake uncovered 10 to 15 minutes or until heated through.

Yield: about 1½ dozen pies

HEART PLACE MATS

For each place mat, you will need 1 purchased rectangular place mat, three 5″ squares of fabric for hearts, paper-backed fusible web, tracing paper, and a black permanent felt-tip pen with fine point.

1. Cut a piece of web slightly smaller than each fabric square. Following manufacturer's instructions, fuse web to wrong side of each square.
2. For heart pattern, follow Transferring Patterns, page 122. Use pattern and cut 1 heart from each fabric square.
3. Arrange hearts along right edge of place mat. Follow manufacturer's instructions to fuse hearts in place.
4. Use pen to draw lines along edge of each heart to resemble stitches.

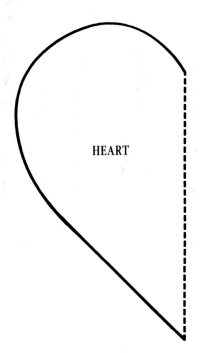

HEART

A friend is one to whom we cling, though many leagues of space separate us.

— J.E. DINGER

Whether near or far, true friends always stick together. To commemorate such a relationship, why not bake a batch of yummy Blueberry Sticky Buns! Topped with a sweet honey-pecan glaze, the rolls are simply bursting with blueberries. A willow basket lined with a crisp blue and white cloth makes a nice carrier for the buns.

BLUEBERRY STICKY BUNS

    3 cups all-purpose flour
    ½ cup granulated sugar
    2 packages active dry yeast
    1 teaspoon salt
 1¼ cups butter or margarine,
         softened and divided
    ½ cup buttermilk
    ¼ cup milk
    1 teaspoon vanilla extract
    2 eggs
    2 cups firmly packed brown sugar,
         divided
    1 cup fresh blueberries
    4 teaspoons ground cinnamon
    1 cup chopped pecans
    ½ cup honey

In a large bowl, combine first 4 ingredients. In a small saucepan, combine 1 cup butter and next 3 ingredients over medium-low heat. Stir until mixture reaches 130 degrees (butter may not be completely melted). Remove from heat; whisk in eggs. Stir egg mixture into dry ingredients; knead until a soft dough forms. Turn dough onto a lightly floured surface. Knead about 5 minutes or until dough becomes elastic and pliable. Form into a ball; place in a greased bowl. Grease top of dough, cover, and refrigerate 2 hours or until well chilled. In a small bowl, stir together 1 cup brown sugar, blueberries, and cinnamon; set aside. In another small bowl, stir together remaining brown sugar, pecans, and honey. Spoon a heaping tablespoon pecan mixture into the bottoms of 12 greased jumbo muffin tins; set aside.

Turn dough onto a lightly floured surface; knead 2 to 3 minutes or until smooth. Using a floured rolling pin, roll out dough to a 10 x 18-inch rectangle. Sprinkle blueberry mixture evenly over dough. Beginning with 1 long edge, roll dough tightly jelly-roll fashion. Cut evenly into 12 slices. Place 1 slice of dough over pecan mixture in each muffin tin. In a small saucepan, melt remaining butter over medium heat. Brush tops of slices with melted butter. Cover and let rise in a warm place (80 to 85 degrees) 1 hour or until doubled in size.

Preheat oven to 350 degrees. Bake 35 to 40 minutes or until golden brown. Turn onto waxed paper to cool completely. Store in an airtight container. Give with serving instructions.

Sticky buns may be served warm or at room temperature. To reheat, preheat oven to 350 degrees. Bake uncovered on a greased baking sheet 3 to 5 minutes or until heated through.

Yield: 1 dozen buns

The best antiques are old friends.

Light, airy Maple Divinity is a delightful, old-fashioned treat for an old friend. To present it, adorn a keepsake box with antique pretties. A treasured photograph of you and your friend will remind her of the good times you've shared.

MAPLE DIVINITY

  2 cups granulated sugar
  ½ cup light corn syrup
  ½ cup water
  ⅛ teaspoon salt
  2 egg whites
  1 teaspoon maple flavoring
  1 cup chopped walnuts

Grease sides of a large stockpot. Combine first 4 ingredients in pot over medium-low heat, stirring constantly until sugar dissolves. Syrup will become clear. Using a pastry brush dipped in hot water, wash down any sugar crystals on sides of pot. Attach candy thermometer to pot, making sure thermometer does not touch bottom of pot. Increase heat to medium and bring to a boil. Do not stir while syrup is boiling.

While syrup is boiling, beat egg whites in a large bowl until stiff using highest speed of an electric mixer.

Continue to cook syrup until it reaches firm ball stage (approximately 242 to 248 degrees). Test about ½ teaspoon syrup in ice water. Syrup will form a firm ball in ice water but will flatten if pressed when removed from water. While beating egg whites at low speed, slowly pour syrup into egg

whites. Add maple flavoring and increase speed of mixer to high. Continue to beat until candy is no longer glossy and a stationary column forms when beaters are lifted. Fold in nuts. Pour into a greased 8-inch square baking dish. Allow to harden. Cut into 1-inch squares. Store in an airtight container.

Yield: about 5 dozen squares divinity

FRIENDSHIP KEEPSAKE BOX

You will need a round Shaker box, doily to cover lid, satin ribbon, a ladies' wrist-length glove, 8″ of florist wire, thread to match glove, a purchased ribbon rose, acrylic paint, foam brush, hot glue gun, glue sticks, and items to

decorate box (we used pearl jewelry, buttons, bits of lace, a handkerchief, and a purchased oval frame with picture inserted).

1. For glove bow on lid, leave thumb of glove free and fanfold glove lengthwise; wrap center securely with wire. Wrap thumb around center of glove, covering wire; tack in place. Tie a length of ribbon into a bow; glue bow to center of glove. Glue ribbon rose over knot of bow.
2. To decorate lid, thread a length of ribbon through doily; center and glue doily to lid. Arrange glove bow and other items on lid until desired effect is achieved; glue in place. Set lid aside.
3. Paint inside and outside of box; allow to dry.

FRIENDSHIP
HATH NO SEASON

This basket makes a lovely friendship gift for any season. Pesto Salad Sprinkles offer crunchy springtime goodness, and Lemon Jelly brings the tart and tangy taste of summer sunshine. While creamy Pumpkin Pudding is a spicy reminder of autumn's bounty, Raspberry Cocoa Mix is a delightful winter warmer. Packed in canning jars with handcrafted lids, they may be given separately or as a group.

PESTO SALAD SPRINKLES

16 slices white bread, lightly toasted
1 package (½ ounce) pesto sauce mix
½ cup butter or margarine, melted
¼ cup olive oil

Preheat oven to 375 degrees. Trim and discard crusts; cut bread into ½-inch cubes. In a large bowl, combine remaining ingredients; stir until well blended. Add bread and toss until well coated. Spread evenly on an ungreased baking sheet. Bake 12 to 15 minutes or until golden brown and crunchy. Store in an airtight container.

Yield: about 4 cups salad sprinkles

LEMON JELLY

8 medium lemons, peeled, seeded, and coarsely chopped
7 cups water
4½ cups granulated sugar
1 box (1¾ ounces) pectin
Yellow food coloring

Combine lemons and water in a large stockpot over medium-high heat. Bring to a boil; reduce heat to medium. Simmer uncovered 45 minutes. Strain fruit mixture, reserving liquid. If necessary, add additional water to reserved liquid to equal 2½ cups. Combine liquid and sugar in stockpot over medium heat; stir until sugar dissolves. Increase heat to medium-high and bring to a rolling boil. Add pectin; stir until dissolved. Bring to a rolling boil again and boil 1 minute longer. Remove from heat; skim off foam. Tint to desired color. Following Sealing Jars instructions, page 120, pour into jars. Store in refrigerator.

Yield: about 3 pints jelly

PUMPKIN PUDDING

2 cups milk
1 box (3 ounces) vanilla pudding mix (do not use instant)
1 can (16 ounces) pumpkin
1 teaspoon pumpkin pie spice

Combine milk and pudding mix in a medium saucepan. Cook over medium heat, stirring constantly, until mixture coats the back of a spoon (about 15 minutes). Remove from heat. Add remaining ingredients; stir until smooth. Store in an airtight container in refrigerator.

Yield: about 3 cups pudding

RASPBERRY COCOA MIX

3 cups instant hot cocoa mix
1 package (0.13 ounces) unsweetened raspberry-flavored soft drink mix

Combine ingredients in a medium bowl; stir until well blended. Store in an airtight container. Give with serving instructions.

To serve, stir 2 heaping tablespoonfuls into 8 ounces hot water.

Yield: about 3 cups cocoa mix

Note: If making decorative jar lid inserts for Seasons Basket (instructions on page 32), store foods in wide-mouth canning jars.

Continued on page 32

SEASONS BASKET

You will need an approx. 8½″ square basket with handle (our basket has 4 sections); tracing paper; graphite transfer paper; four 6″ squares of canvas fabric; black permanent felt-tip pen with fine point; watercolor markers (see color keys for colors); small paintbrush; paper towels; craft batting; lightweight cardboard; craft glue; a 10¾″w wooden banner cutout (available at craft stores); beige acrylic paint; foam brush; artificial snow; artificial leaves, grass, and flowers; hot glue gun; and glue sticks.

1. For jar lid inserts, trace patterns onto tracing paper. Use transfer paper to transfer 1 design to center of each canvas square.

2. (*Note:* Practice coloring technique on scrap canvas before coloring jar lid inserts.) Refer to photo, page 30, and color keys to color designs. To blend colors, dip paintbrush in water; remove excess water on a paper towel until brush is almost dry. Brush over colored areas of design. Repeat as desired. Allow to dry.

3. Follow Jar Lid Finishing, page 122, to complete each jar lid insert.

4. Place snow, leaves, grass, and flowers in basket. Place jars in basket.

5. Paint banner cutout beige. Allow to dry.

6. Use black pen to write ''FRIENDSHIP HATH NO SEASON'' on banner. Hot glue banner to basket handle.

SPRING
Outline and detail lines - permanent black
Flower - yellow, lt purple, purple, and dk purple
Leaves - green and dk green

SUMMER
Outline and detail lines of sun - permanent black
Sun - yellow, dk yellow, and orange

WINTER
Outline of snowflake - dk blue

AUTUMN
Outline and detail lines of acorn - permanent black
Outline of leaf - dk orange
Detail lines of leaf - permanent black
Acorn - brown and tan
Leaf - yellow, dk yellow, orange, dk orange, and red

Heaven gives us friends to bless the present scene.
— EDWARD YOUNG

This dreamy Seventh Heaven Layered Salad will be a blessing for a busy friend who's hosting a luncheon or dinner party. The seven layers are created with fresh vegetables, grated cheese, and a lightly seasoned creamy dressing; crumbled bacon atop the salad adds a flavorful finishing touch. A clear glass trifle bowl provides a taste-tempting view of the appealing treat. Later, your friend will find many uses for the lovely dish.

SEVENTH HEAVEN LAYERED SALAD

DRESSING

- 1 package (8 ounces) cream cheese, softened
- 1 cup mayonnaise
- 1 cup sour cream
- 1 teaspoon dried ground basil leaves
- ½ teaspoon garlic powder
- ½ teaspoon onion powder

SALAD

- ½ head iceberg lettuce, chopped
- 2 large tomatoes, chopped
- 1 large cucumber, sliced
- 4 large carrots, peeled and sliced
- 10 green onions, finely chopped
- 2 cups (8 ounces) grated sharp Cheddar cheese
- 1 pound bacon, cooked and crumbled

For dressing, combine all ingredients in a medium bowl; blend well using medium speed of an electric mixer. Cover and set aside.

For salad, layer vegetables and cheese in desired order in a trifle bowl or large glass container. Spread dressing evenly over vegetables. Garnish with crumbled bacon. Cover and store in refrigerator.

Yield: about 10 servings

33

Scrumptious Trillionaire Candy will be a luxurious indulgence for a lucky friend! Unbelievably easy to make, the sweet treats are created by coating butter crackers with a rich concoction of golden caramel, dark chocolate, and crunchy pecans. A gleaming brass basket festooned with shiny coins makes a splendid carrier for the candy.

TRILLIONAIRE CANDY

- 1 container (12½ ounces) caramel topping
- 1 cup finely chopped pecans
- 3 dozen round butter-flavored crackers
- 1 package (12 ounces) semisweet chocolate chips

In a medium saucepan, combine caramel topping and pecans over medium heat. Stirring constantly, bring to a boil and cook 3 to 5 minutes longer or until mixture thickens. Remove from heat and allow to cool 5 minutes. Spoon about 1½ teaspoons caramel mixture on top of each cracker. Refrigerate 1 hour or until firm. In a small saucepan, melt chocolate chips over low heat, stirring constantly. Remove from heat. Using tongs, dip bottom of each cracker in chocolate. Transfer to waxed paper and refrigerate 1 hour or until chocolate is firm. Store in an airtight container in refrigerator.

Yield: 3 dozen candies

34

Of all the heavenly gifts that mortal men commend, what trusty treasure in the world can countervail a friend?

— NICHOLAS GRIMALD

When you need an extra-nice remembrance for a dear friend, our Raspberry Angel Food Cake is heaven-sent. The delicate cake features a creamy raspberry frosting and lots of fresh berries. This elegant, easy-to-make dessert will put your favorite diner on cloud nine.

RASPBERRY ANGEL FOOD CAKE

CAKE
- 1 package (12 ounces) frozen raspberries, thawed
- 1 purchased angel food cake (9-inch diameter)

FROSTING
- 1 package (8 ounces) cream cheese, softened
- 2 cups confectioners sugar
- 2 tablespoons sour cream
- 2 tablespoons crème de cassis liqueur
  Red food coloring (optional)
  Fresh raspberries for garnish (optional)

Drain thawed raspberries, reserving juice. Cut cake in half horizontally; remove top layer. Spoon raspberries evenly over bottom layer of cake. Reserving 2 tablespoons juice for frosting, pour remaining juice evenly over raspberries on cake. Replace top layer of cake.

For frosting, beat cream cheese until fluffy using medium speed of an electric mixer. Add reserved juice and next 3 ingredients; stir until well blended. If desired, tint with food coloring. Transfer ½ cup frosting to a pastry bag fitted with a large star tip. Spread remaining frosting on sides and top of cake. Pipe a decorative border along bottom and top edges of cake. If desired, garnish with fresh raspberries. Store in an airtight container in refrigerator.

Yield: about 16 servings

Life just isn't the same when a friend moves away — even if it's just across town. Presented in a blue sponge-painted crock, this Blue Cheese Dressing is an affectionate way to say, "I miss you." The spicy vinaigrette dressing is made with olive oil and seasoned with red wine vinegar, garlic, green onions, and Dijon mustard. A bowl of salad fixings is a fresh way to round out your gift.

BLUE CHEESE DRESSING

- ¾ cup olive oil
- ¼ cup red wine vinegar
- 3 tablespoons Dijon-style mustard
- 2 green onions, finely chopped
- 1 teaspoon garlic powder
- 1 teaspoon salt
- ½ teaspoon ground black pepper
- 4 ounces blue cheese, crumbled

In a blender or a food processor fitted with a steel blade, process first 7 ingredients until smooth. Transfer to a small bowl; stir in cheese. Cover and chill 8 hours or overnight to allow flavors to blend. Store in an airtight container in refrigerator.

Yield: about 1½ cups salad dressing

SPONGE-PAINTED CROCK

You will need desired light-colored crock, blue enamel model paint, small piece of cellulose sponge, paper for label, blue felt-tip calligraphy pen with medium point, and craft glue.

1. (*Note:* If desired, practice painting technique on paper before painting crock.) Use sponge piece to lightly stamp blue paint on outside of crock, allowing color of crock to show through; allow to dry.
2. For label, use pen to write "BLUE CHEESE DRESSING" on paper. Draw a box around lettering. Trim label to desired size. Glue label to crock; allow to dry.

When we love, it is the heart that judges.

Brighten a favorite friend's day by presenting her with a hearty loaf of homemade bread topped with a blue ribbon in honor of your friendship! This savory Onion-Pecan Bread, with its unusual combination of pecans and red onions, is sure to please. Your thoughtful gesture will make her feel like a winner!

ONION-PECAN BREAD

   3 cups all-purpose flour
   1 package active dry yeast
1½ teaspoons granulated sugar
1½ teaspoons salt
   ¾ cup finely chopped pecans
   ½ cup finely chopped red onion
   1 cup plus 1 tablespoon milk
   ¼ cup butter

Sift first 4 ingredients together in a large bowl. Stir in pecans and onion. In a small saucepan, combine milk and butter over medium-low heat. Stir occasionally until milk mixture reaches 130 degrees (butter may not be completely melted). Stir milk mixture into dry ingredients; knead until a soft dough forms.

Turn dough onto a lightly floured surface. Knead about 5 minutes or until dough becomes elastic and pliable. Form into a ball. Place dough in a greased bowl, grease top of dough, and cover. Let rise in a warm place (80 to 85 degrees) 1 hour or until doubled in size. Turn dough onto a lightly floured surface and punch down. Form into a loaf shape and transfer to a greased 5 x 9-inch loaf pan. Grease top of dough and cover. Let rise in a warm place 1 hour or until doubled in size.

Preheat oven to 375 degrees. Bake 35 to 40 minutes or until golden brown. Invert onto a wire rack to cool completely. Store in an airtight container.

Yield: 1 loaf bread

PRIZE RIBBON

You will need 1¼ yds of 1⅝"w blue satin ribbon, blue thread, a 2½" dia. circle of white medium weight cardboard, blue felt-tip calligraphy pen with fine point, 1" long pin back, hot glue gun, and glue sticks.

1. Cut a 28" length from ribbon. Matching right sides, use a ¼" seam allowance to sew ends together; press seam allowance to 1 side.
2. Baste ¼" and ⅛" from 1 long edge of ribbon. Pull basting threads, drawing up gathers to a 2" dia. circle; knot threads and trim ends.
3. Use pen to write "1st Prize Friend" on cardboard circle.
4. Glue cardboard circle to center of gathered ribbon circle.
5. For streamers, cut remaining ribbon in half. Glue 1 end of each streamer to back of cardboard circle. Cut a V-shaped notch in each streamer.
6. Glue pin back to back of cardboard circle.

A friend may well be reckoned the masterpiece of nature.

— RALPH WALDO EMERSON

Crowned with a wreath of Marzipan Fruit, this masterpiece will be a breathtaking tribute to your best friend. The rich Vanilla Wafer Cake features a luscious blend of vanilla, coconut, and pecan flavors. Nestled atop the creamy frosting, the realistic fruit is sculpted from a sweet confection of ground almonds. To present this work of art, we covered a cake box with elegant wrapping paper and tied it with a golden ribbon.

VANILLA WAFER CAKE WITH MARZIPAN FRUIT

MARZIPAN FRUIT
- 1⅓ cups slivered almonds, finely ground
- 3⅔ cups confectioners sugar, divided
- 3 tablespoons water
- 1 teaspoon almond extract
- Peach, purple, red, green, orange, yellow, and brown paste food coloring
- 1-inch cinnamon sticks
- Whole cloves
- Water

CAKE
- ¾ cup butter or margarine, softened
- 1½ cups granulated sugar
- 6 eggs
- 2 teaspoons vanilla extract
- 1 box (12 ounces) vanilla wafer cookies, finely crushed
- ½ cup milk
- 1 cup finely chopped pecans
- 1⅓ cups sweetened grated coconut

FROSTING
- 2 packages (8 ounces each) cream cheese, softened
- 1 cup butter or margarine, softened
- 3 tablespoons milk
- 4 teaspoons vanilla extract
- 8 cups confectioners sugar

Note: Make marzipan fruit 1 day in advance of making cake.

For marzipan fruit, combine almonds, 1⅓ cups sugar, water, and almond extract; beat until well blended using medium speed of an electric mixer. Beat in remaining sugar. Divide marzipan evenly into 4 small bowls. Tint 1 bowl peach, 1 bowl purple, 1 bowl red, and 1 bowl light green by kneading in food coloring. For each peach, shape about 2 tablespoons peach marzipan into a ball. Make a crease in ball with a knife to resemble a peach. Insert a cinnamon stick in crease for stem; insert a clove in bottom of peach. For each plum, use about 2 tablespoons purple marzipan and repeat instructions for shaping peaches. For each grape, shape about 1 teaspoon red marzipan into a ball. Place several balls together to form a cluster. Insert a cinnamon stick in top of cluster. For each pear, shape about 2 tablespoons green marzipan into a pear shape. Insert a clove in top of pear. In a small bowl, mix a small amount of purple food coloring with water to make a thin paint. Repeat with red, green, orange, yellow, and brown food coloring. To shade fruit, use a small round paintbrush to lightly brush desired diluted food colorings onto fruit. Cover with plastic wrap and refrigerate.

Preheat oven to 350 degrees. For cake, cream butter and sugar in a large bowl until fluffy. Add eggs 1 at a time, beating well after each addition. Beat in vanilla. Add cookie crumbs and milk alternately to creamed mixture. Fold in pecans and coconut. Spoon batter into a greased and floured 9-inch springform tube pan. Bake 1 hour 10 minutes to 1 hour 15 minutes or until a toothpick inserted in cake comes out clean. Cool in pan 10 minutes; remove sides of pan. Invert onto a wire rack to cool completely.

For frosting, combine first 4 ingredients in a large bowl. Add sugar and beat until smooth. Use ½ of frosting to frost sides and top of cake.

For basketweave technique, transfer remaining frosting to a pastry bag fitted with a basketweave tip. With serrated side of tip up, pipe a vertical stripe of frosting from top edge to bottom edge of cake. Pipe three 1-inch long horizontal stripes over vertical stripe about 1 tip width apart (Fig. 1).

Fig. 1

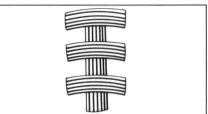

Overlapping ends of horizontal stripes, pipe another vertical stripe to the right of the first vertical stripe (Fig. 2a). Pipe two 1-inch long horizontal stripes as shown in Fig. 2b. Repeat basketweave technique until side of cake is covered. Using a large star tip, pipe decorative border along bottom edge of cake.

Fig. 2a

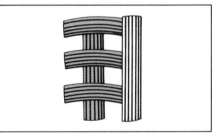

Fig. 2b

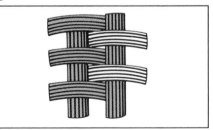

Arrange marzipan fruit, silk leaves, and grape tendrils on top of cake. Store in an airtight container in refrigerator.

Yield: about 20 servings

For box, follow Gift Box 2 instructions, page 123. We used a 10″ cake box and decorated it with 1½″ wide ribbon.

The road to a friend's house is never long.

Show a friend who's near or far how much you appreciate her with a basket of Stenciled Grahams. To make the crispy treats, we used food coloring to add a homey motif to store-bought graham crackers. A set of matching kitchen towels will be a lasting reminder of your friendship.

STENCILED GRAHAMS

- 1 box (16 ounces) graham crackers
- 1 tablespoon powdered or paste red food coloring
- 1 tablespoon water

Break graham crackers into squares. In a small bowl, stir food coloring and water together until smooth. Using food coloring, follow How To Stencil, page 122, to stencil house design on crackers. Store in an airtight container.

Yield: about 5 dozen crackers

KITCHEN TOWELS

For each towel, you will need 1 approx. 14½" x 22" kitchen towel with area suitable for stenciling (we used a Charles Craft® Ecru Color-Effects™ towel); fabric for bias trim strips; thread to match fabric; tracing paper; graphite transfer paper; tagboard (manila folder); craft knife; cutting mat or a thick layer of newspapers; removable tape (optional); stencil brushes; red, green, and brown fabric paint; and paper towels.

1. Wash, dry, and press towel.
2. Draw a 2¼" square on tracing paper.
3. Follow Step 1 of How To Stencil, page 122, to make a stencil for square. Repeat to make a stencil for house and trees design.
4. Follow Step 2 of How To Stencil, page 122, to stencil brown square at center of towel insert. Centering house over brown square, repeat to stencil house and trees.

5. Follow paint manufacturer's instruction to heat-set design if necessary.
6. For bias trim strips, cut two 1½" wide bias strips from fabric 1" longer than width of towel. Press edges of each strip ½" to wrong side. Pin 1 strip along top edge of towel insert; pin remaining strip along bottom edge of insert. Stitching close to edges of each strip, sew strips in place.

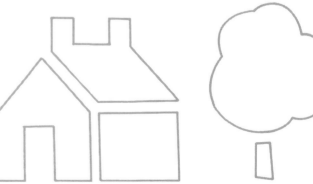

40

A day for toil, an hour for sport, But for a friend is life too short.

— RALPH WALDO EMERSON

With today's hectic lifestyles, it's important to make time for your friends. Our Salmon Pot Pie will save a friend some time in the kitchen so the two of you can enjoy a visit. The hearty one-dish meal features chunks of salmon and vegetables in a creamy sauce. Just for fun, we topped the flaky crust with a clock face.

SALMON POT PIE

CRUST

2 cups all-purpose flour
1 teaspoon salt
⅔ cup vegetable shortening
6 tablespoons cold water

FILLING

2 tablespoons vegetable oil
2 salmon steaks (about 10 ounces)
1 teaspoon salt, divided
½ teaspoon ground black pepper, divided
3 tablespoons all-purpose flour
1 teaspoon garlic powder
1 teaspoon dried rosemary, crushed
2 cups milk
2 cans (16 ounces each) mixed vegetables, drained
1 egg, beaten
Brown and red paste food coloring
2 tablespoons water, divided

For crust, sift together flour and salt in a medium bowl. Using a pastry blender or 2 knives, cut shortening into flour mixture until mixture resembles coarse meal. Sprinkle water over. Knead until a soft dough forms. On a lightly floured surface, use a floured rolling pin to roll out ⅔ of dough to ¼-inch thickness. Transfer rolled dough to a 1½-quart round casserole (dough will drape over sides of dish). Cover casserole and remaining dough with plastic wrap.

Preheat oven to 400 degrees. For filling, heat oil in a large skillet over medium heat. Sprinkle salmon evenly with ½ teaspoon salt and ¼ teaspoon pepper. Place salmon in skillet and cook until flaky, turning once. Transfer to paper towels. Add remaining salt and pepper and next 3 ingredients to skillet; stir to make a paste. Gradually add milk; stir until smooth. Stir in vegetables. Stirring constantly, bring to a boil; cook 3 to 5 minutes or until sauce thickens. Remove skin and bones from fish. Break into pieces and stir into sauce. Pour filling into crust. Fold edges of crust over filling. Brush edges with egg. On a lightly floured surface, use a floured rolling pin to roll remaining dough to ¼-inch thickness. For top crust, use a sharp knife to cut a circle ¼-inch smaller than diameter of casserole; reserve dough scraps. Place crust over filling. Using a sharp knife, score top crust to resemble clock face. For clock hands, follow Transferring Patterns, page 122. Place patterns on dough scraps and use a sharp knife to cut out clock hands and center of dial. Brush backs of cutouts with egg. Arrange on crust. In a small bowl, mix brown food coloring and 1 tablespoon water to make a thin paste; repeat with red food coloring. Use a clean paintbrush to brush brown food coloring on hands; repeat to brush red food coloring on center of dial. Bake 45 to 50 minutes or until brown. Cool completely on a wire rack. Place plastic numbers on pie. Cover and refrigerate until ready to present. Give with serving instructions.

To serve, preheat oven to 350 degrees. Remove numbers from pie. Cover and bake 25 to 30 minutes or until heated through.

Yield: about 8 servings

Friendship warms the heart.

When winter's chill is in the air, a gift of hot and spicy White Chili will warm hearts — and tummies, too! The hearty chili is made with chicken and great northern beans for a delicious variation of a favorite cold weather recipe. Our little "heartwarming" basket is just right for delivering the chili.

WHITE CHILI

- 2 tablespoons vegetable oil
- 1 medium white onion, finely chopped
- 1 can (4 ounces) chopped green chilies
- 2 teaspoons garlic powder
- 2 teaspoons salt
- 2 teaspoons ground cumin
- 2 teaspoons ground oregano
- 2 teaspoons ground coriander
- ½ teaspoon cayenne pepper
- 2 cans (15.8 ounces each) great northern beans (do not drain)
- 2 cans (10½ ounces each) chicken broth
- 2 cans (5 ounces each) chicken, drained

In a large stockpot, heat oil over medium heat. Add onion; sauté until brown. Add next 7 ingredients; stir until well blended. Stir in remaining ingredients. Bring to a boil; reduce heat to low. Simmer 15 to 20 minutes or until heated through. Store in an airtight container in refrigerator. Give with serving instructions.

To serve, transfer chili to a large stockpot. Cook over medium heat 10 to 15 minutes or until heated through.

Yield: 8 to 10 servings

HEARTWARMING BASKET

You will need desired basket, one 5″ square of unbleached muslin fabric for heart, four 5″ squares of fabric for mittens, thread to match mitten fabric, two ½″ x 3¼″ strips of artificial lamb fleece, tracing paper, fabric marking pencil, craft batting, lightweight cardboard, polyester fiberfill, craft glue, red permanent felt-tip pen with fine point, 26″ of cotton string, large needle, hot glue gun, glue sticks, fabric to cover jar lid, and ribbon the width of side of lid.

1. (*Note:* Use craft glue unless otherwise indicated.) For heart pattern, follow Transferring Patterns, page 122. Use pattern and cut 1 heart from cardboard and 1 from batting.
2. Use fabric marking pencil to draw around pattern on muslin. Use red pen to write "FRIENDSHIP WARMS THE HEART" in heart on muslin. Cut out heart ½″ larger than drawn line.

3. Place muslin heart right side down. Center batting heart, then cardboard heart, on muslin heart. At ½″ intervals, clip edge of muslin to ⅛″ from cardboard. Pulling muslin taut, glue cut edges of muslin to top (back) of cardboard heart.
4. Leaving top edges open, use mitten pattern and follow Transferring Patterns and Sewing Shapes, page 122, to make 2 mittens; do not turn mittens right side out. Trim top of each mitten along pencil line. Turn mittens right side out. Stuff bottom half of each mitten lightly with fiberfill. Glue top of each mitten closed.
5. With ends of strip at back of each mitten, glue 1 fleece strip around top edge of each mitten for cuff.
6. Cut string in half. Use needle to thread 1 length through top edge of each mitten at thumb side.
7. Hot glue heart to basket. Hot glue 1 mitten to each side of heart and to basket. Thread 1 end of each string through basket rim and tie into a bow; knot ends of string.
8. For jar lid, use fabric marking pencil to draw around lid on wrong side of fabric. Cut out circle ½″ larger than drawn line. At ½″ intervals, clip fabric to ⅛″ from drawn line. Using lid as a pattern, cut a circle from batting. Glue batting to lid. Center fabric circle right side up on lid. Pulling fabric taut, glue clipped edges of fabric to side of lid. Cut ribbon ½″ longer than circumference of lid. Glue ribbon to side of lid, covering edges of fabric.

MITTEN

Leave Open

HEART

43

Friendship is Love without his wings!

— LORD BYRON

These light, airy Angel Biscuits are an exquisite way to surprise a friend! Sweetened coconut gives the fluffy biscuits a delicate flavor. Perched on the gift basket, a pair of gilded cherubs blow playful kisses to your friend. A bow of satin ribbons graces the basket handle, and floral fabric makes a pretty liner.

ANGEL BISCUITS

2½ cups biscuit baking mix
½ cup sweetened shredded coconut
1 cup whipping cream
2 tablespoons butter or margarine, melted

Preheat oven to 450 degrees. In a large bowl, combine baking mix and coconut. Add cream and stir until well blended. Turn dough onto a lightly floured surface and knead about 1 minute. Use a floured rolling pin to roll out dough to ½-inch thickness. Use a floured 2-inch biscuit cutter to cut out dough. Place biscuits 2 inches apart on a greased baking sheet and brush tops with melted butter. Bake 7 to 10 minutes or until light brown. Transfer to a wire rack to cool completely. Store in an airtight container. Give with serving instructions.

To serve, preheat oven to 350 degrees. Cover and bake 3 to 5 minutes or until heated through.

Yield: about 1½ dozen biscuits

CHERUB BASKET

You will need a basket with handle, desired ribbon, 2 small plaster cherubs (available at craft stores), metallic gold spray paint, hot glue gun, glue sticks, fabric for liner, and thread to match fabric.

1. Spray paint cherubs gold; allow to dry.
2. Tie ribbon lengths together into a bow. Glue bow to center top of basket handle. Arrange streamers around handle; glue to secure. Glue 1 cherub to handle over bow.
3. For liner, cut a square from fabric ½" larger on all sides than desired finished size. Press edges of fabric ¼" to wrong side; press ¼" to wrong side again and stitch in place. Place liner in basket. Set remaining cherub on rim of basket.

The sweetness of a summer rose garden is deliciously captured in our Rose Petal Jam. Created with dewy-fresh rose petals, the unique preserves have a delightful honey-like flavor. For a feminine gift, trim a jar of the jam with floral fabric and satin ribbon and present it in a pretty basket. Freshly picked roses make a lovely finishing touch.

ROSE PETAL JAM

- 1⅔ cups granulated sugar
- 1⅓ cups water
- 2 cups firmly packed fragrant rose petals from pesticide-free blossoms (about 15 large roses), washed
- 1 teaspoon rose flower water (available at gourmet food stores)
- 1 box (1¾ ounces) pectin Red food coloring (optional)

In a large stockpot, combine sugar and water over medium-high heat; stir constantly until sugar dissolves. Stir petals and rose flower water into syrup. Bring to a rolling boil. Add pectin; stir until dissolved. Bring to a rolling boil again and boil 1 minute longer. Remove from heat; skim off foam. If desired, tint with food coloring. Following Sealing Jars instructions, page 120, pour into jars. Store in refrigerator.

Yield: about 1 pint jam

For jar lid, follow Jar Lid Finishing, page 122. For trim on lid, cut a 1½″ wide fabric strip 2″ longer than circumference of lid. Press edges of strip ½″ to wrong side. Glue strip to side of lid. Cut a length of ¼″ wide ribbon ½″ longer than circumference of lid. Glue ribbon to side of lid.

Old tunes are sweetest, old friends are surest.

Flash back to the fifties with this rockin' gift! Loaded with tuna, almonds, and rice in a creamy sauce, hearty "Tune-A" Amandine Casserole is a tasty version of a golden oldie. To carry the dish in style, we painted a serving basket bubble gum pink and added paper music notes just for fun. A pair of record-shaped potholders given with the casserole is sure to be a hit!

"TUNE-A" AMANDINE CASSEROLE

- 2 tuna steaks (about 1¼ pounds)
- 1 teaspoon salt, divided
- ½ teaspoon ground black pepper, divided
- 2 tablespoons vegetable oil
- ½ cup sliced almonds
- ¼ cup butter or margarine
- 1 large onion, chopped
- 3 tablespoons all-purpose flour
- 2 cups milk
- 2 cups cooked rice
- 1 lemon, cut into thin slices (for garnish)

Rinse tuna steaks with cold water; pat dry with paper towels. Sprinkle both sides of tuna steaks evenly with ½ teaspoon salt and ¼ teaspoon pepper. In a large skillet, heat oil over medium heat. Add tuna steaks and cook until brown and flaky, turning once. Transfer to paper towels to drain; set aside. Add next 3 ingredients to oil in skillet; sauté until onion is tender.

Sprinkle flour and remaining salt and pepper evenly over onion mixture; stir until well blended. Continue to cook until flour begins to brown. Gradually stir in milk. Stirring constantly, bring to a boil and cook 3 to 5 minutes or until sauce thickens. Remove from heat.

Spoon rice into a 3-quart casserole. Break tuna steaks into pieces and place over rice. Pour sauce evenly over tuna. Garnish with sliced lemon. Cover and refrigerate until ready to present. Give with serving instructions.

To serve, preheat oven to 350 degrees. Cover and bake 25 to 30 minutes or until heated through.

Yield: 6 to 8 servings

To decorate basket for casserole, paint basket pink; allow to dry. Trace note pattern onto tracing paper; cut out. Use pattern and cut notes from black paper. Glue notes to basket.

RECORD POTHOLDERS

For each potholder, you will need two 10″ squares and one 1½″ x 28″ bias strip of black fabric for record, one 6″ square of fabric for label, thread to match fabrics, fusible craft batting, paper-backed fusible web, and a black permanent felt-tip pen with fine point.

1. For label appliqué, cut a piece of web slightly smaller than label fabric square. Following manufacturer's instructions, fuse web to wrong side of fabric.
2. Cut a 4″ dia. circle from label fabric square. Cut a 1¼″ dia. circle from center of 4″ dia. circle and discard.
3. Following manufacturer's instructions, center and fuse label to right side of 1 black fabric square (top).
4. Use a medium width zigzag stitch with a short stitch length and thread to match label fabric to appliqué label to top square.
5. Cut 2 pieces from batting slightly smaller than remaining black fabric square (bottom). Following manufacturer's instructions, fuse both batting pieces to wrong side of square.
6. Cut a piece of web slightly smaller than top square. Following manufacturer's instructions, fuse web to wrong side of square.
7. With label centered, cut an 8″ dia. circle from top square. Fuse circle to center of batting side of bottom square.
8. Stitching through all layers, topstitch ½″, 1″, and 1¾″ from outer edge of label. Trim batting and bottom square even with top.
9. For binding, match wrong sides and fold bias strip in half lengthwise; press. Fold long edges to center; press.
10. Insert raw edges of potholder between folded edges of binding. Stitching close to inner edge of binding, sew binding to potholder; continue stitching to end of binding. Referring to Fig. 1, form a loop from end of binding. Whipstitch end to back of potholder.

Fig. 1

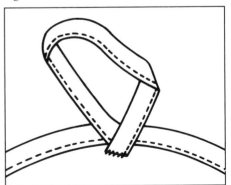

11. Use pen to write "OLD TUNES ARE SWEETEST, OLD FRIENDS ARE SUREST" on label.

The best gifts are tied with heartstrings.

This simple gift is guaranteed to tug at the heartstrings of a dear friend! Two surprise ingredients — ramen noodles and sunflower seeds — lend a crisp, nutty flavor to our Crunchy Cheese Ball while green onions and parsley add a touch of color. To deliver the gift, tuck the treat, along with some crackers, into a fabric-lined basket. Attaching little painted hearts to bows of cotton string is a sentimental (and quick!) way to decorate the basket.

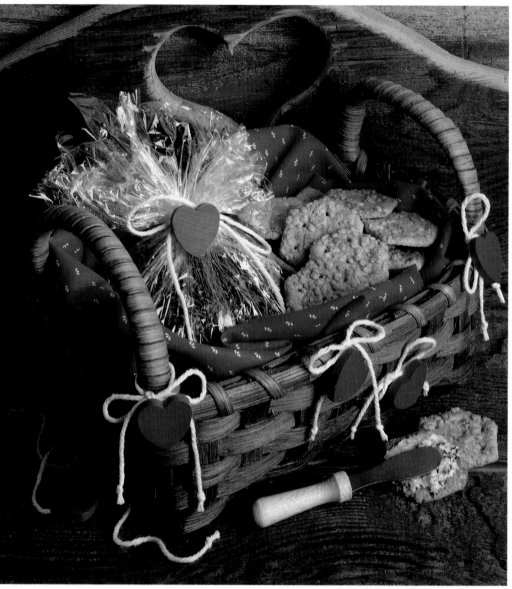

CRUNCHY CHEESE BALL

- 1 package (3 ounces) chicken-flavored ramen noodle soup
- 2 packages (8 ounces each) cream cheese, softened
- 1 cup sour cream
- ½ cup dry-roasted shelled sunflower seeds
- 4 green onions, chopped
- ⅓ cup dried parsley flakes

In a food processor fitted with a steel blade, process noodles, contents of seasoning packet, and next 4 ingredients until well blended. Divide mixture in half. Shape each half into a ball. Roll in parsley. Wrap in plastic wrap and refrigerate. Give with serving instructions.

To serve, let stand at room temperature 20 to 30 minutes or until softened. Serve with crackers or bread.

Yield: 2 cheese balls

For basket, cut 12″ lengths from cotton string. Tie 1 length into a bow around plastic wrap on cheese ball; thread remaining lengths through basket or around basket handle and tie into bows. Knot end of each streamer. Use craft glue to glue a red 1″ wide wooden heart cutout to 1 streamer of each bow. Line basket with a fabric square.

Two lovely berries moulded on one stem: So, with two seeming bodies, but one heart.

— WILLIAM SHAKESPEARE

Here's an appealing gift for a friend who's a lot like you. Two-Berry Jam, with its twin combination of blackberries and raspberries, has a sweet fruity flavor that's perfect with biscuits or English muffins. Just the right size to hold a pint jar of the jam, our little basket is decorated with lifelike berries and a cheerful raffia bow.

TWO-BERRY JAM

1 cup frozen blackberries, thawed
  and drained
1 cup frozen raspberries, thawed
  and drained
4 cups granulated sugar
1 package (3 ounces) liquid pectin

In a large stockpot, combine first 3 ingredients over medium-high heat. Bring to a rolling boil, stirring constantly until sugar dissolves. Stir in pectin. Bring to a rolling boil again and boil 1 minute longer. Remove from heat; skim foam from top. Following Sealing Jars instructions, page 120, fill jars. Store in refrigerator.

Yield: about 2 pints jam

BERRY BASKET

You will need a small round basket with handle, artificial raspberries and blackberries, raffia, hot glue gun, glue sticks, excelsior, lightweight cardboard, craft batting, a 4″ square of fabric, and craft glue.

1. Arrange berries along handle and rim on 1 side of basket; hot glue to secure. Tie raffia into a bow; hot glue bow to basket.
2. For jar lid insert, follow Jar Lid Finishing, page 122. Fill basket with excelsior; place jar in basket.

49

When I give to you what I make with my hands, I share my heart.

A spicy cake decorated with a nostalgic crazy-quilt motif is a sentimental way to show a close friend that she holds an important place in your heart. A pleasing combination of coffee, oatmeal, and spices gives this moist cake a wonderful flavor that is as special as your friendship. The homey patchwork heart is easily made with icing tinted in soft country colors. Created with love, the design reminds us of a handmade quilt — carefully pieced together over time, much like the friendship this simple gift celebrates.

Preheat oven to 350 degrees. For cake, use medium speed of an electric mixer to mix first 4 ingredients together in a large bowl; set aside for 15 minutes. In another large bowl, sift together next 6 ingredients. Using medium speed of mixer, beat butter mixture until fluffy. Add eggs 1 at a time, beating well after each addition. Add dry ingredients to creamed mixture; beat until well blended. Fold in walnuts. Pour batter into a greased and floured 8-inch square baking pan. Bake 40 to 45 minutes or until a toothpick inserted in center comes out clean. Cool in pan 10 minutes; turn onto a wire rack to cool completely.

For icing, combine sugar and milk in a large bowl; beat until smooth. Divide 2 cups icing evenly between 4 small bowls. Tint 1 light pink, 1 pink, 1 light blue, and 1 blue. Cover tinted icings and set aside. Spread remaining white icing on sides and top of cake. Allow icing to harden. To transfer pattern to top of cake, trace pattern onto tracing paper. Center pattern on top of cake and use a toothpick to punch holes about ¼-inch apart through pattern into icing. Remove pattern. Referring to photo, spread light pink and light blue icing inside heart design on cake. Allow icing to harden. Referring to photo for details, use a pastry bag fitted with a small round tip to pipe pink dots on top of light pink icing. Using a pastry bag fitted with a very small round tip, pipe light pink plaid design on top of light blue icing. Using a pastry bag fitted with a small round tip, pipe light blue lines inside heart design on cake. Using a pastry bag fitted with a small round tip, pipe blue icing along edge of heart design to resemble stitches. Allow icing to harden. Store in an airtight container.

Yield: 10 to 12 servings

SPICY HEART CAKE

CAKE

  1 cup firmly packed brown sugar
  1 cup quick-cooking rolled oats
  1 cup brewed coffee
  ¾ cup butter or margarine, softened
  1 cup all-purpose flour
  1 teaspoon baking soda
  1 teaspoon ground cinnamon
  ½ teaspoon baking powder
  ½ teaspoon salt
  ½ teaspoon ground allspice
  2 eggs
  ½ cup finely ground walnuts

ICING

  6 cups confectioners sugar
  ½ cup plus 1 tablespoon milk
  Pink and blue paste food coloring

Friendship multiplies our joy and divides our grief.

Just as a friendship grows and brings pleasure over the years, so will a gift of Sourdough Starter provide continuing delight to a friend. The starter makes it easy to enjoy the fresh-baked goodness of our Sourdough Molasses Bread anytime — and your friend can use it in other sourdough recipes, too. For a sampling of the good tastes to come, place a loaf of the bread in a basket with the starter and recipe.

SOURDOUGH STARTER

  2 cups warm milk
  2 cups all-purpose flour
  1 package active dry yeast

Combine all ingredients in a very large non-metal container; stir until well blended. Loosely cover with cheesecloth and let stand in a warm place (80 to 85 degrees) 24 hours. Give with recipe for Sourdough Molasses Bread and instructions for replenishing.

To replenish starter, stir in equal amounts of flour and warm water (80 to 85 degrees) to replace the mixture used. (For example, if 1 cup starter is used, replace with ½ cup flour and ½ cup warm water.) Let stand in a warm place at least 24 hours before using. If starter is not used every 3 to 5 days, remove 1 cup starter and replenish as directed. Store loosely covered in refrigerator. Bring to room temperature before using.

Yield: about 4 cups starter

SOURDOUGH MOLASSES BREAD

  8 cups all-purpose flour, divided
  2 cups warm water
  2 cups warm milk
  1 cup Sourdough Starter
  1 tablespoon butter or margarine, melted
  1 package active dry yeast
  1 cup whole wheat flour
  ½ cup granulated sugar
  ¼ cup molasses
  2 teaspoons salt
  2 teaspoons baking soda

In a large bowl, combine 2½ cups all-purpose flour and next 4 ingredients.

Stir in yeast and set aside 30 minutes. Add wheat flour and next 4 ingredients; stir until well blended. Gradually add remaining all-purpose flour; knead until a soft dough forms. Turn dough onto a lightly floured surface; knead until dough becomes pliable and elastic. Shape dough into 4 loaves and place in greased 5 x 9-inch loaf pans. Grease tops of loaves. Let rise in a warm place (80 to 85 degrees) 1 hour or until doubled in size.

Preheat oven to 350 degrees. Bake 25 to 30 minutes or until brown. Transfer to a wire rack to cool completely. Store in an airtight container.

Yield: 4 loaves bread

These realistic Acorn Cookies are perfect for a fall friendship gift! Accented with chocolate, nuts, and a clove "stem," the almond treats are sweetened with brown sugar and spiced with cinnamon. A basket decorated in rich autumn colors is a fitting way to present the cookies.

ACORN COOKIES

  1 cup butter or margarine, softened
1½ cups firmly packed brown
     sugar
  1 teaspoon almond extract
  1 envelope unflavored gelatin
  2 tablespoons hot water
  2 cups all-purpose flour
  ½ teaspoon ground cinnamon
  ¼ teaspoon salt
3¼ cups finely ground almonds
  1 cup (6 ounces) semisweet
     chocolate chips
  1 cup finely chopped almonds
    Whole cloves

Preheat oven to 375 degrees. In a large bowl, cream butter and sugar until fluffy. Beat in almond extract. In a small bowl, dissolve gelatin in water. Add to creamed mixture; stir until well blended. In a medium bowl, sift together next 3 ingredients. Add dry ingredients to creamed mixture; stir until a soft dough forms. Fold in ground almonds. Shape dough into 1-inch diameter acorn shapes. Transfer to a greased baking sheet. Bake 10 to 12 minutes or until light brown. Transfer to a wire rack to cool completely.

Melt chocolate chips in a small saucepan over low heat; remove from heat. Dip wide end of each cookie in chocolate; roll chocolate-dipped end in chopped almonds. For stem, insert the round end of 1 clove into the chocolate-dipped end of each cookie. Allow chocolate to harden. Store in an airtight container.

Yield: about 6 dozen cookies

If friends were flowers, I'd pick you.

These Apricot Flower Cookies look like real blossoms, especially when arranged in flowerpots like ours! Shaped in a candy mold and decorated to resemble black-eyed Susans, the chewy cookies are made with apricot preserves for a sweet, fruity flavor. "Leaves" cut from green paper can be used as tags to personalize the cookies. You can give a friend a whole pot of these sunny "flowers" — or present them individually as treats.

APRICOT FLOWER COOKIES

½ cup butter or margarine, softened
1 cup firmly packed brown sugar
½ cup granulated sugar
1 egg
1 teaspoon vanilla extract
½ cup apricot preserves
3 cups all-purpose flour
¼ teaspoon salt
   Wooden skewers
   Yellow and brown paste food
      coloring
2 tablespoons water, divided
   Purchased chocolate-flavored
      decorating icing

In a large bowl, cream butter and sugars until fluffy. Add egg and vanilla; beat until smooth. Beat in preserves. In a medium bowl, sift flour and salt together. Add dry ingredients to creamed mixture; knead until a soft dough forms. Cover and chill 30 minutes.

Preheat oven to 350 degrees. For each cookie, press about 1 tablespoon dough into a greased 3-inch flower-shaped candy mold. Invert mold onto a greased baking sheet and press on mold to release dough. Insert a skewer into bottom of each cookie. Bake 12 to 15 minutes or until brown. Transfer to a wire rack to cool completely.

In a small bowl, combine yellow food coloring and 1 tablespoon water; stir until smooth. Use a small paintbrush to brush yellow food coloring on each cookie. Allow to dry. In another small bowl, combine brown food coloring and remaining water; stir until smooth. Use a small paintbrush to paint details on petals of each cookie. Allow to dry. Using a small star tip, pipe icing in center of each cookie. Allow to dry. Store in an airtight container.

Yield: about 3½ dozen cookies

POTTED COOKIES

For each pot, you will need desired flowerpot, a block of floral foam to fill pot to 1″ from rim, green excelsior, desired ribbon, green paper for tag, tracing paper, black felt-tip pen with fine point, and craft glue.

1. Place floral foam in pot. Fill pot to rim with green excelsior, covering foam.
2. To decorate pot with ribbon, glue ribbon around rim of pot; tie ribbon into a bow around skewer of 1 flower; or glue ribbon around rim of pot and glue a bow made from several lengths of ribbon to rim.
3. Inserting skewers into foam, arrange desired number of cookies in pot.
4. For tag, trace leaf pattern onto tracing paper; cut out. Use pattern and cut tag from green paper. Use pen to write name on tag. Fold square end of tag ½″ to wrong side; glue folded end of tag around skewer of 1 cookie. Glue additional leaves to skewers if desired.

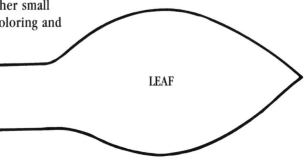

LEAF

ℛeep thy friend under thy own life's key.
— WILLIAM SHAKESPEARE

Because friends are the key to a happy life, we keep them close to our hearts. Presented with a heart-shaped key chain, creamy Key Lime Pie conveys this sentiment to someone special. The glittery handmade key chain displays your unique selection of shiny sequins and trinkets.

KEY LIME PIE

CRUST

   1½ cups all-purpose flour
   ½ teaspoon salt
   ½ cup vegetable shortening
   ¼ cup cold water

FILLING

   4 egg yolks
   1 can (14 ounces) sweetened
      condensed milk
   ⅓ cup freshly squeezed lime juice
      (juice of about 3 limes)
      Green food coloring (optional)

MERINGUE

   4 egg whites
   ½ teaspoon cream of tartar
   ½ cup granulated sugar

   Preheat oven to 450 degrees. For crust, sift flour and salt together in a medium bowl. Using a pastry blender or 2 knives, cut in shortening until mixture resembles coarse meal. Sprinkle water over; mix until a soft dough forms. On a lightly floured surface, use a floured rolling pin to roll out dough to ⅛-inch thickness. Transfer to a 9-inch pie plate and use a sharp knife to trim edges of

dough. Prick crust with a fork. Bake 8 minutes. Cool completely on a wire rack.

   Reduce oven temperature to 325 degrees. For filling, combine egg yolks, condensed milk, and lime juice in a medium saucepan over low heat. Cook, stirring constantly, until mixture reaches 160 degrees (about 10 minutes). Remove from heat. If desired, tint green.

   For meringue, beat egg whites and cream of tartar in a large bowl until foamy using highest speed of an electric mixer. Gradually add sugar; beat until stiff peaks form.

   Pour filling into crust. Spread meringue evenly over filling. Bake 25 to 30 minutes or until meringue is brown. Cool completely on a wire rack. Cover and refrigerate until ready to present.

Yield: 8 to 10 servings

HEART KEY CHAIN

You will need a 2″w plastic heart-shaped mold (we used a plaster of paris mold; available at craft stores), gold mesh key chain hardware and a ⅝″ dia. jump ring (available at craft stores), high gloss clear epoxy coating (we used Aristocrat™ Epoxy Thick Crystal Clear Coating), and desired sequins and charms.

1. (*Note:* Read all epoxy coating instructions before beginning.) Arrange 1 layer of sequins and charms in bottom of mold. Carefully following manufacturer instructions, pour a layer of coating into mold, covering sequins and charms. Continue adding sequins and coating to mold until mold is filled to rim. Immerse ⅔ of jump ring into coating at top of heart. Allow coating to harden completely

2. Press back of mold to remove heart. Attach key chain hardware to jump ring.

A meal becomes a feast when shared with friends.

Shared with a good friend at work, this simple meal becomes a fun indoor picnic! Tortellini Salad features purchased cheese-filled pasta and chunks of pepperoni in a spicy marinade, and the crispy Orange Thins make a light, tasty dessert. An old-fashioned lunch box painted with bright designs is a cute way to package the feast.

ORANGE THINS

 ½ cup butter or margarine, softened
 ½ cup granulated sugar
 1 tablespoon frozen orange juice concentrate, thawed
 ½ teaspoon vanilla extract
 ½ teaspoon orange-flavored extract
 ½ teaspoon dried grated orange peel
 1 cup all-purpose flour
 ¼ teaspoon salt
 ½ cup chopped walnuts

Preheat oven to 350 degrees. In a large bowl, cream butter and sugar until fluffy. Add next 4 ingredients; mix until smooth. In a blender or food processor fitted with a steel blade, process remaining ingredients until walnuts are finely ground. Add dry ingredients to creamed mixture; stir until a soft dough forms. Shape into ½-inch balls and place 2 inches apart on a greased baking sheet. Flatten each ball with a spatula. Bake 8 to 10 minutes or until brown. Transfer to a wire rack to cool completely. Store in an airtight container.

Yield: about 3 dozen cookies

TORTELLINI SALAD

 2 packages (9 ounces each) refrigerated cheese-filled tortellini (we used spinach and plain tortellini)
 6 ounces pepperoni, cut into pieces
 ¾ cup olive oil
 ½ cup white wine vinegar
 6 green onions, coarsely chopped
 3 tablespoons chopped fresh parsley
 1 tablespoon garlic salt
 2 teaspoons dried crushed basil
 1 teaspoon salt
 ¼ teaspoon ground black pepper

Cook tortellini according to package directions. Drain and rinse with cold water. Transfer tortellini to a large bowl; add pepperoni. In a blender or food processor fitted with a steel blade, process remaining ingredients until well blended. Pour oil mixture over tortellini mixture; toss until well coated. Cover and refrigerate 8 hours or overnight to allow flavors to blend.

Yield: 8 to 10 servings

For lunch box, we used shiny dimensional paint in squeeze bottles to paint wavy lines, swirls, and dots on a purchased lunch box.

A home-made friend wears longer than one you buy in the market.

— AUSTIN O'MALLEY

A homemade gift is always extra special, and our Blackberry Chutney is better than anything you could find in a store! The tangy concoction of berries, celery, and onion is lightly sweetened with honey and spiced with cinnamon for a delightfully different condiment. Cradling a jar of chutney, our pinafore-clad bear looks like a much-loved companion — but she's really a new bear who's been given a time-worn look.

BLACKBERRY CHUTNEY

2 tablespoons hot water
1 teaspoon unflavored gelatin
1 tablespoon vegetable oil
¼ cup finely chopped celery
2 tablespoons finely chopped onion
1 package (16 ounces) frozen
    blackberries, thawed
¼ cup red wine vinegar
3 tablespoons honey
2 tablespoons granulated sugar
½ teaspoon ground cinnamon

In a small bowl, combine water and gelatin; stir until dissolved. In a medium saucepan, heat oil over medium heat. Add celery and onion; sauté until tender. Add remaining ingredients; stir until well blended. Bring to a boil; remove from heat. Stir gelatin mixture into blackberry mixture. Following Sealing Jars instructions, page 120, fill jar. Store in refrigerator. Serve with meat or bread. Include serving suggestions with gift.

Yield: about 1 pint chutney

OLD FRIEND BEAR

For bear, you will need a 12"h purchased stuffed teddy bear, 2 old unmatched buttons for eyes, thread to sew on buttons, yarn for nose and mouth, large needle, dk brown waterbase stain, foam brush, craft glue, and cream-type cosmetic blush.

For clothing, you will need a 6" x 30" piece of unbleached muslin fabric, one 1½" x 30" bias strip and one 2" x 36" bias strip of fabric for apron ties, one 2" square of fabric for heart, paper-backed fusible web, tracing paper, two ⅜" dia. buttons, thread to match muslin and bias strips, coordinating embroidery floss, an approx. 5"w straw doll bonnet, and ⅔ yd of ⅞"w ribbon.

1. Use a seam ripper, scissors, or pliers to remove eyes and nose from bear. If necessary, sew up holes where eyes and nose were. Sew old buttons to bear for eyes. Use yarn and a satin stitch to stitch a new nose; use straight stitches to stitch a new mouth.
2. To make fur look old, apply stain unevenly over fur. Allow to dry.
3. To mat fur together, use fingers to work craft glue into small areas. Allow to dry.
4. Apply blush to cheeks.
5. For apron, cut two 3¾" x 2⅝" pieces from muslin for bib and a 6" x 20" piece from muslin for skirt.
6. For bib, match edges and place muslin pieces together. Use a ⅜" seam allowance to sew 1 long edge and 2 short edges together. Cut corners diagonally, turn right side out, and press.
7. For skirt, press short edges of muslin ¼" to 1 side (wrong side); press ¼" to wrong side again and stitch in place. Press 1 long raw edge (bottom) 1¼" to wrong side. Using a 1" seam allowance and a long running stitch, hem bottom edge of skirt using 2 strands of floss. Baste ¼" and ⅛" from remaining raw edge (top) of skirt. Pull basting threads, gathering top edge of skirt to 10"; knot and trim basting threads.
8. For ties at waist and neck, match wrong sides and fold each bias strip in half lengthwise; press. Fold long edges of each strip to center and press.
9. For waistband and ties, center gathered edge of skirt between folded edges of 36" long strip, leaving 13" of strip at each end; pin in place. Beginning at 1 end of fabric strip, sew close to folded edges of strip.
10. With right side of bib facing wrong side of waistband and waistband overlapping raw edge of bib ½", center edge of bib under waistband. Stitching close to top edge of waistband, sew waistband to bib.
11. For ties at neck, sew close to folded edges of remaining strip; cut strip in half. Press 1 end of each tie ½" to 1 side (wrong side). Sew pressed ends of ties and buttons to top corners of bib.
12. For heart, cut a piece of web slightly smaller than fabric piece. Follow manufacturer's instructions to fuse web to wrong side of fabric. Trace heart pattern onto tracing paper; cut out. Use pattern and cut heart from fabric. Fuse heart to bib.
13. Place apron on bear and tie waist and neck ties into bows. Place bonnet on bear's head; tie ribbon into a bow around bonnet and head to secure.

Friendship endures forever.

Just as a golden ring symbolizes never-ending love, our Ring of Gold Apricot Cake will be a sweet reminder of the enduring bond you share with a special friend. Sour cream and apricot jam give the dessert a rich flavor and moist texture. This delicious token of your esteem is sure to be appreciated.

RING OF GOLD APRICOT CAKE

CAKE

- 1 cup butter or margarine, softened
- 2 cups granulated sugar
- 5 eggs
- ½ cup apricot jam
- ½ cup sour cream
- 1 teaspoon vanilla extract
- 2 cups all-purpose flour
- 1 teaspoon baking soda
- ½ teaspoon salt
- 2 cups sweetened shredded coconut
- 1 cup finely chopped pecans
- 1 package (8 ounces) dried apricots, finely chopped

GLAZE

- ½ cup apricot jam
- 2 tablespoons apricot nectar

Preheat oven to 350 degrees. For cake, cream butter and sugar in a large bowl until fluffy. Add eggs 1 at a time, beating well after each addition. Stir in next 3 ingredients. In a medium bowl, sift together next 3 ingredients. Stir dry ingredients into creamed mixture. Fold in remaining ingredients. Pour batter into a greased and floured 10-inch tube pan. Bake 45 to 55 minutes or until a toothpick inserted in center comes out clean. Cool in pan 10 minutes; turn onto a wire rack to cool completely.

For glaze, combine jam and nectar in a small saucepan over medium heat; stir until well blended. Pour evenly over top of cake. Store in an airtight container.

Yield: about 20 servings

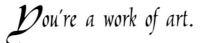

A color photocopy of a famous painting transforms this ordinary tin into a work of art! It's sure to please an exceptional friend, especially when filled with our Curried Pretzels. To make the crunchy snack, we added a spicy coating to ready-made pretzels. Your friend will think this gift is a real masterpiece!

CURRIED PRETZELS

- 1 bag (10 ounces) Bavarian pretzels
- 3 tablespoons butter or margarine
- ½ teaspoon curry powder
- ¼ teaspoon seasoned salt

Preheat oven to 225 degrees. Place a single layer of pretzels on a baking sheet. In a small saucepan, melt butter over medium heat. Add remaining ingredients; stir until well blended. Using a pastry brush, brush butter mixture on each pretzel. Bake 20 to 25 minutes or until dry to the touch. Cool completely on pan. Store in an airtight container.

Yield: about 2½ dozen pretzels

ARTFUL GIFT TIN

You will need a color photocopy (we used a copy of a photograph of a painting), a tin with lid large enough to accommodate photocopy, flat black spray paint, desired gold trim, spray adhesive, craft glue, and tissue paper to line tin.

1. Spray paint outside of tin and lid black. Allow to dry.
2. Trim photocopy to fit top of lid. Use spray adhesive to glue photocopy to lid.
3. Place lid on tin. Use craft glue to glue trim around sides of tin just below lid. Allow to dry.
4. Line tin with tissue paper.

During the cool, crisp days of autumn, a jar of rich, spicy Pumpkin Butter will be a pleasant surprise for a dear friend. Our reusable papier mâché pumpkin container is a cute way to present the sweet spread — and it makes an attractive fall accent, too.

PUMPKIN BUTTER

4½ cups granulated sugar
1 can (16 ounces) pumpkin
1 tablespoon pumpkin pie spice
1 box (1¾ ounces) pectin

In a large saucepan, combine first 3 ingredients over medium heat; stir constantly until sugar dissolves. Bring to a rolling boil. Add pectin; stir until dissolved. Bring to a rolling boil again and boil 1 minute longer. Remove from heat; skim off foam. Following Sealing Jars instructions, page 120, pour into jars. Store in refrigerator. Serve with bread or muffins. Include serving suggestions with gift.

Yield: about 2 pints pumpkin butter

Note: If making pumpkin jar, store pumpkin butter in a half-pint canning jar.

PUMPKIN JAR

You will need a half-pint canning jar (same size as jar used in recipe), lightweight cardboard, masking tape, aluminum foil, instant papier mâché (we used Celluclay® Instant Papier Mâché), resealable plastic bag (optional), gesso, green and burnt orange acrylic paint, dk brown waterbase stain, foam brushes, a soft cloth, fabric to cover jar lid, craft batting, craft glue, green cloth-covered florist wire, green Paper Capers™ twisted paper, tracing paper, hot glue gun, glue sticks, waxed paper, and matte clear acrylic spray.

Note: To store pumpkin butter, remove jar from papier mâché pumpkin.

1. Cut a 2¾" x 10" strip and a 4½" dia. circle from cardboard. Overlapping short edges, wrap strip around side of jar; tape to secure.
2. Leaving top and bottom of cardboard tube open, wrap and crush foil pieces around tube, forming a 5½" dia. pumpkin shape; press indentations into foil to resemble pumpkin (Fig. 1). Pumpkin should be well shaped and firm before papier mâché is added.

Fig. 1

5½"

3. (*Note:* Keep fingers wet when working with papier mâché. Excess papier mâché can be stored in a resealable plastic bag in refrigerator for up to 4 days.) Follow manufacturer's instructions to mix instant papier mâché with water. Apply a ⅛" to ¼" thick layer of papier mâché over pumpkin shape. On a piece of waxed paper, form an approximately 1" high pumpkin stem from papier mâché. Allow papier mâché to dry completely. Remove jar from pumpkin.
4. Center cardboard circle on bottom of pumpkin; trim circle to fit if necessary. Use craft glue to glue circle to bottom of pumpkin. Allow to dry.
5. Remove screw ring from filled jar of pumpkin butter, being careful not to break seal. If seal of jar is broken, refrigerate jar. Apply 1 coat of gesso and 1 coat of burnt orange paint to pumpkin and screw ring, allowing to dry between coats. Repeat to paint stem green.
6. Apply stain to pumpkin, screw ring, and stem; wipe off excess with soft cloth. Allow to dry. Apply 1 coat of acrylic spray to pumpkin, screw ring, and stem. Allow to dry.
7. Trace leaf patterns onto tracing paper; cut out. Use patterns and cut 1 of each leaf from untwisted Paper Capers™.
8. For tendrils, wrap two 12" lengths of wire around a pencil; slide pencil out.
9. For fabric-covered jar lid insert, follow Jar Lid Finishing, page 122. Place jar of pumpkin butter in pumpkin. Hot glue leaves, tendrils, and stem to top of jar lid.

Dear friends are not forgotten, they live within your heart.

When a dear friend is moving away, remind her to keep in touch with a linen-lined basket of Forgotten Cookies. The delightfully crisp meringue treats are enhanced with chopped pecans. Given with the cookies, a photo album covered with dainty handkerchiefs and lace is a lovely place to store pictures of the two of you.

FORGOTTEN COOKIES

   1 cup chopped pecans
   4 egg whites
   ½ teaspoon cream of tartar
   1 cup sifted confectioners
        sugar
   2 teaspoons vanilla extract

Preheat oven to 350 degrees. Spread pecans evenly on an ungreased baking sheet. Stirring occasionally, bake 10 to 15 minutes. Remove from oven; cool to room temperature.

Reduce oven temperature to 200 degrees. In a large bowl, beat egg whites until foamy. Add cream of tartar; beat until soft peaks form. Gradually add sugar, beating until stiff peaks form. Stir in vanilla. Fold in pecans. Drop by tablespoonfuls onto a waxed paper-lined baking sheet. Bake 2 hours 30 minutes to 2 hours 40 minutes or until golden yellow. Cool completely on baking sheet. Carefully peel away waxed paper. Store in an airtight container.

Yield: about 3½ dozen cookies

PHOTO ALBUM

You will need a purchased small white photo album; desired lace, ribbon, bows, and handkerchiefs; white fabric for lining; craft batting; lightweight cardboard; fabric glue; hot glue gun; and glue sticks.

1. For padded front, measure front of album. Cut cardboard and batting ¼″ smaller on all sides than album front. Cut lining fabric ¾″ larger on all sides than album front.
2. Arrange lace, ribbon, bows, and pieces cut from handkerchiefs on lining; use fabric glue to secure. Allow to dry. Trim lace, ribbon, and handkerchief pieces even with edge of lining.

3. Place lining on a flat surface with decorated side down. Center batting then cardboard on lining. Pulling fabric taut, hot glue edges of fabric to back of cardboard. Hot glue lace around edge of padded front. Center padded front on album front; hot glue to secure.
4. To decorate spine of album, cut a handkerchief piece same size as spine. Press any raw edges ¼″ to wrong side; use fabric glue to secure. Center handkerchief piece on spine; use fabric glue to secure. Cut lengths of lace and ribbon same width as handkerchief piece. Tie a length of ribbon into a bow. Arrange lace, ribbon lengths, and bow on handkerchief piece; use fabric glue to secure. Allow to dry.

They are rich who have true friends.

— THOMAS FULLER

Here's a wonderful treat for a true friend! Garnished with almonds, our rich Chocolate-Filled Butter Cake has a delicious chocolate filling nestled between two layers of moist, melt-in-your-mouth cake. We chose a pretty floral paper napkin to create our decoupage serving plate, then added gold trim around the edge. This beautiful gift will be a lasting reminder of the richness of your friendship.

CHOCOLATE-FILLED BUTTER CAKE

CAKE

- ½ cup butter or margarine, softened
- ⅓ cup firmly packed brown sugar
- ¼ cup milk
- 1½ teaspoons vanilla extract
- 1 cup all-purpose flour
- ⅛ teaspoon salt

FILLING

- ¼ cup semisweet chocolate chips
- 1 tablespoon butter or margarine

   Whole almonds for garnish

Preheat oven to 350 degrees. In a large bowl, cream butter and sugar until fluffy. Add milk and vanilla; mix until well blended. In a medium bowl, sift together flour and salt. Add dry ingredients to creamed mixture; stir until well blended.

For filling, melt chocolate chips and butter in a medium saucepan over low heat; stir until smooth. Remove from heat. Spread ½ of batter evenly into a greased and floured 7-inch springform pan. Spread filling evenly over batter. Spread remaining batter over filling. Place almonds on top of batter. Bake 40 to 45 minutes or until edges are brown. Cool in pan 10 minutes; transfer to a wire rack to cool completely. Store in an airtight container.

Yield: about 6 servings

DECORATIVE PLATE

You will need a 9″ dia. clear glass plate, ⅛″w gold braid trim, ¼″w gold gimp trim, a printed paper napkin with design area at least 8¾″ square, matte Mod Podge® sealer, and foam brush.

Note: Plate is for decorative use only. Wipe clean with a damp cloth.

1. On back of plate, use sealer to glue right side of braid ⅛″ from edge of plate; glue gimp to back of plate just inside braid. Allow to dry.
2. Unfold napkin. Cut an 8¾″ dia. circle from printed area of napkin. Circle should be 1 printed layer of napkin; if necessary, separate layers of napkin.
3. Apply sealer to back of plate. Center napkin circle right side down on back of plate. Beginning at center, press circle onto plate, flattening wrinkles to form a smooth surface. Allow to dry.
4. Apply 2 coats of sealer to back of plate, allowing to dry between coats.

Colorful jelly beans make this candy extra special! A traditional brittle recipe with a sweet surprise instead of peanuts, our Jelly Bean Brittle is sure to bring smiles to youngsters, especially when it's presented in a bright, happy clown bag. For fun party favors, make a bag and fill it with brittle for each child.

Jelly Bean Brittle

1½ cups jelly beans
3 cups granulated sugar
1 cup light corn syrup
½ cup water
3 tablespoons butter or margarine
1 teaspoon salt
2 teaspoons baking soda

Spread jelly beans evenly on greased aluminum foil. Grease sides of a large stockpot. Combine next 3 ingredients over medium-low heat; stir constantly until sugar dissolves. Using a pastry brush dipped in hot water, wash down any sugar crystals on sides of pot. Attach candy thermometer to pot, making sure thermometer does not touch bottom of pot. Increase heat to medium and bring to a boil. Do not stir while syrup is boiling. Continue to cook syrup until it reaches hard crack stage (approximately 300 to 310 degrees) and turns golden brown. Test about ½ teaspoon syrup in ice water. Syrup should form brittle threads in ice water and remain brittle when removed from water. Remove from heat and add butter and salt; stir until butter melts. Add soda (syrup will foam); stir until soda dissolves. Pour syrup over jelly beans. Using 2 greased spoons, pull edges of warm candy until stretched thin. Cool completely on foil. Break into pieces. Store in an airtight container.

Yield: about 2 pounds brittle

Clown Bag

You will need 1 approx. 6″ x 11″ yellow gift bag, fabric for hat, fabric for ruffle, thread to match ruffle fabric, pinking shears, tracing paper, white paper, red paper, white pencil, 1″ dia. rubber ball, 2 jacks, a 1¾″ dia. pom-pom, a ¾″ dia. pom-pom, a 6″ long chenille stem, curly doll hair (available at craft stores), hot glue gun, and glue sticks.

1. For hat, cut a piece from fabric 4¼″ high and the width of front of bag. Trim 1 long edge (bottom edge) with pinking shears. Matching top and side edges, glue fabric piece to front of bag.

2. For ruffle, cut a strip from fabric 6″ wide and twice as long as width of front of bag. Matching wrong sides, fold strip in half lengthwise; press. Baste ½″ and ¼″ from raw edge. Pull basting threads, drawing up gathers to 2″ wider than front of bag; knot basting threads and trim ends. Press short edges of ruffle ½″ to 1 side (wrong side); press gathered edge ½″ to wrong side. Glue pressed gathered edge to bag.
3. Trace eye, flower, and mouth patterns onto tracing paper; cut out. Use patterns and cut 2 eyes and 1 flower from white paper and 1 mouth from red paper.
4. Draw a white line along center of mouth. Glue mouth and eyes to bag. Glue rubber ball to bag for nose. Glue 1 jack to each eye.
5. Cut two 12″ long bunches from hair. Knot center of each bunch. Glue knot of 1 bunch to each side of bag at bottom edge of hat. Trim hair as desired.
6. Place a plastic bag of candy in bag. Fold top corners of bag diagonally to back to form point of hat. Glue 1¾″ dia. pom-pom to point.
7. For flower, glue ¾″ dia. pom-pom to center of flower. Glue flower to 1 end of chenille stem. Glue remaining end of stem to hat.

$\mathcal{A}$ true friend is the gift of God, and he only who made hearts can untie them.

— ROBERT SOUTH

Baked in the shape of a traditional symbol of unity, our Honey-Buttermilk Bread is a special treat for a true friend. The delicious yeast bread is lightly sweetened with honey and flavored with just a hint of almond. Our attractive bread tray is easy to make from a picture frame — just choose a pretty fabric to display beneath the glass and add handles for carrying. It's a handsome accessory that can be used for years to come.

HONEY-BUTTERMILK BREAD

- 3 cups all-purpose flour
- 1½ teaspoons salt
- 1 package active dry yeast
- ¾ cup buttermilk
- ½ cup warm water
- 3 tablespoons honey
- 1 tablespoon butter or margarine, melted
- 1 teaspoon almond-flavored extract

In a large bowl, stir together first 3 ingredients. In a medium bowl, whisk together remaining ingredients. Add buttermilk mixture to dry ingredients; knead until a soft dough forms. Turn dough onto a lightly floured surface; knead about 5 minutes or until dough becomes soft and pliable. Place in a greased bowl; grease top of dough. Cover and let rise in a warm place (80 to 85 degrees) 1 hour or until doubled in size. Turn dough onto a lightly floured surface and punch down. Divide dough in half; shape each half into an 18-inch long log shape. Pinch together ends of 1 log shape to form a ring; transfer to a greased baking sheet. Interlocking 1 ring with the other, repeat with remaining log shape. Grease top of dough. Cover and let rise in a warm place 1 hour or until doubled in size.

Preheat oven to 350 degrees. Bake 30 to 35 minutes or until golden brown. Transfer to a wire rack to cool completely. Store in an airtight container.

Yield: 1 loaf bread

PICTURE FRAME TRAY

You will need desired size plain wooden picture frame, 2 cabinet handles with screws, 2 pieces of medium weight cardboard and 1 piece of glass to fit frame, desired fabric, glazier's points (available at craft or hardware stores), a ⅛″ thick sheet of cork same size as frame, hot glue gun, and glue sticks.

1. Use screws to attach cabinet handles to opposite sides on front of frame.
2. Cut fabric 1″ larger on all sides than 1 piece of cardboard. Center cardboard on wrong side of fabric. Pulling fabric taut, glue edges of fabric to top (wrong side) of cardboard.
3. Insert glass, fabric-covered cardboard, and remaining cardboard piece into frame. Use glazier's points to tightly secure glass and cardboard in frame.
4. Trim cork to ⅛″ smaller than tray on all sides. Center and glue cork to bottom of tray.

journeyed to the rainbow's end, and found not gold — but you, my friend.

A good friend is more valuable than the pot of gold at the end of the rainbow. And a jar of our Rainbow Fruit Salad is a nice way to tell someone, "That's how I feel about you." The cool, refreshing salad features kiwifruit, strawberries, mandarin oranges, and pineapple in a creamy lemon dressing. It's a great treat for summertime — or anytime! Adorned with a rainbow of ribbons and a sprinkling of golden coins, a wooden bucket makes a colorful presentation.

RAINBOW FRUIT SALAD

- 1 can (14 ounces) sweetened condensed milk
- ¼ cup frozen lemonade concentrate, thawed
- 1 can (16 ounces) mandarin oranges, drained
- 1 can (20 ounces) pineapple chunks, drained
- 2 kiwifruit, peeled and sliced
- 1 pint strawberries, capped and sliced

In a large bowl, stir together condensed milk and lemonade using medium speed of an electric mixer. Add remaining ingredients; stir by hand until fruit is well coated. Store in an airtight container in refrigerator.

Yield: about 10 servings

RAINBOW BUCKET

You will need a wooden bucket (available at craft or import stores), white paint, foam brush, desired ribbon, gold coin charms (available at craft stores), fabric glue, hot glue gun, glue sticks, and tissue paper.

1. Paint bucket white; allow to dry.

2. Use fabric glue to glue lengths of ribbon to front of bucket; trim ribbon ends even with top and bottom edges of bucket. Allow to dry.

3. Tie lengths of ribbon together into bows.

4. Hot glue coin charms and bows to bucket.

5. Line bucket with tissue paper.

If thou require a soothing friend, Forget me not, forget me not!
— AMELIA OPIE

A soothing cup of tea served in a restful spot is a delightful way to unwind after a hectic day. Spiced with cinnamon and nutmeg, this fruity blend is a mixture of lemon, orange, and cherry flavors. A ribbon-tied bag makes a pretty package for the instant mix. Adorned with delicate forget-me-nots — traditional symbols of remembrance — a painted wooden tray will make your gift unforgettable.

FORGET-ME-NOT TEA

- 1 jar (15 ounces) instant orange breakfast drink mix
- 1 cup granulated sugar
- 1 cup unsweetened instant tea mix
- ½ cup presweetened lemonade mix
- 1 package (0.14 ounces) unsweetened cherry-flavored soft drink mix
- 2 teaspoons ground cinnamon
- 1 teaspoon ground nutmeg

In a large bowl, combine all ingredients; mix well. Store in an airtight container. Give with serving instructions.

To serve, stir 2 heaping tablespoons tea mix into 8 ounces hot or cold water.

Yield: about 4 cups tea mix

FORGET-ME-NOT TRAY

You will need a wooden tray (we used a 12″ x 17″ tray); masking tape; tracing paper; graphite transfer paper; white, yellow, lt blue, blue, dk blue, lt green, green, brown, and metallic gold acrylic paint; blue permanent felt-tip pen with fine point; paper towels; paintbrushes; and matte clear acrylic spray.

1. Apply 2 coats of white paint to tray, allowing to dry between coats.
2. For border, refer to Fig. 1 and use tape (shown in grey) to mask off a ½″ wide line 1″ from sides on inside of tray.

Fig. 1

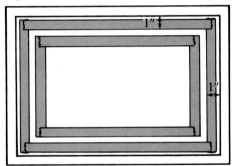

3. Paint border brown; allow to dry. Crumple a small piece of paper towel. Dip towel into gold paint; remove excess on another paper towel. Dipping towel into paint as needed, lightly stamp gold paint over brown paint on border. Allow to dry. Carefully remove tape.
4. Trace "forget-me-not" and flower patterns onto tracing paper.
5. Centering words at each end of border, use transfer paper to transfer words onto tray. Use blue pen to draw over words.
6. Use transfer paper to transfer flower pattern to tray as desired.
7. Use a small round paintbrush to paint flowers lt blue. While paint is still wet, use a clean paintbrush and blue paint to shade petals of each flower. Allow to dry. Use dk blue paint and a liner paintbrush to paint detail lines on each flower. Allow to dry. Use yellow paint to paint each flower center. Allow to dry.
8. Use a small flat paintbrush and lt green paint to paint leaves around flowers as desired. While paint is still wet, use a clean paintbrush and green paint to shade each leaf. Allow to dry.
9. Use a liner paintbrush and gold paint to paint lines connecting flowers and shadows of lettering. Allow to dry.
10. Allowing to dry between coats, apply 2 coats of acrylic spray to tray.

For fabric bag, use a 6½″ x 24″ piece of fabric and follow Steps 2 and 4 of Fabric Bag instructions, page 122. Press top edge of bag 2″ to wrong side. Place a plastic bag of tea mix in bag. Tie 18″ lengths of ⅛″ and ¼″ wide ribbon together into a bow around top of bag.

forget-me-not

$\mathcal{W}$ater your friendships like you water your flowerpots.

Friendships, like flowers, often flourish with a little extra attention, and a close chum will love this perky gift! Crunchy Onion-Sesame Snack Mix is a tasty combination of crackers and peanuts with a zesty coating. A plastic watering can blooming with fabric flowers makes a pretty container for the treat. Later, it can be used as a vase, and the little scoop will make a handy kitchen or garden tool!

ONION-SESAME SNACK MIX

  3 cups oyster crackers
  2 cups dry-roasted peanuts
  ½ cup butter or margarine
  1 package (1 ounce) dry onion
      soup mix
  ¼ cup sesame seeds

Preheat oven to 350 degrees. In a large bowl, combine crackers and peanuts. In a small saucepan, melt butter over medium heat. Remove from heat; stir in remaining ingredients. Pour over cracker mixture; toss until well coated. Spread evenly on a baking sheet. Bake 10 to 12 minutes or until light brown. Cool completely in pan. Store in an airtight container.

Yield: about 5 cups snack mix

WATERING CAN

You will need a watering can (we used a plastic watering can), floral fabric, matte Mod Podge® sealer, and foam brush.

1. Cut desired motif from fabric. Use sealer to glue motif to front of can. Allow to dry.
2. Apply 2 coats of sealer to front of can, allowing to dry between coats.

*W*hen a friend asks, there is no tomorrow.

— GEORGE HERBERT

When a friend needs a little attention, the heart tells us to respond immediately. With these delicious No-Bake Brownies, it's easy to create a thoughtful treat, even when your time is short. A purchased gift bag is a lovely (and quick!) way to package your surprise.

NO-BAKE BROWNIES

   1 can (14 ounces) sweetened
      condensed milk
   1 box (12 ounces) vanilla wafer
      cookies, finely crushed
   ½ cup chopped walnuts
   1 ounce unsweetened chocolate,
      melted
   ½ cup semisweet chocolate chips,
      melted

In a large bowl, mix first 4 ingredients together until well blended using lowest speed of an electric mixer. Spread mixture evenly into a greased 9-inch diameter cake pan. Spread melted chocolate chips over top. Cover and refrigerate 1 hour or until firm. Cut into wedges to serve. Store in an airtight container in refrigerator.

Yield: about 10 to 12 brownies

Love bakes good cakes and brews good stews.

A friend who's fond of homestyle cooking will love this Southern gift box! Easy to prepare, our Black-Eyed Pea Soup is loaded with chunks of pepper, tomato, onion, and bacon. Teamed with traditional Johnny Cakes, the spicy dish makes a wholesome meal. Fabric hearts and letters glued to the wooden carrier proclaim that this gift is ''homemade'' with love.

BLACK-EYED PEA SOUP

6 slices bacon
1 large onion, finely chopped
1 clove garlic, minced
1 teaspoon salt
½ teaspoon ground black pepper
1 can (4 ounces) mild chopped green chilies
4 cans (15.8 ounces each) black-eyed peas
2 cans (14½ ounces each) beef broth
1 can (10 ounces) diced tomatoes and green chilies

In a large stockpot, cook bacon over medium heat until crisp. Transfer to paper towels to drain; crumble bacon. Add next 5 ingredients to bacon drippings in pot; sauté until onion is brown. Add bacon and remaining ingredients. Increase heat to medium-high and bring to a boil. Remove from heat. Store in an airtight container in refrigerator. Give with serving instructions.

To serve, transfer soup to a stockpot. Cook over medium-high heat 10 to 15 minutes or until heated through, stirring occasionally. Serve with Johnny Cakes (recipe follows).

Yield: 12 to 14 servings

JOHNNY CAKES

1 cup all-purpose flour
1 cup cornmeal
4 teaspoons baking powder
1 teaspoon salt
½ teaspoon baking soda
1 egg
1½ cups buttermilk
¼ cup butter or margarine, melted
1½ cups (6 ounces) grated sharp Cheddar cheese
½ cup vegetable oil

In a large bowl, stir together first 5 ingredients. In a medium bowl, whisk together next 3 ingredients. Add egg mixture to dry ingredients; stir just until moistened. Fold in cheese.

In a large skillet, heat oil over medium heat. Drop tablespoonfuls of batter into hot oil. Turning once, cook 3 to 4 minutes or until brown. Transfer to paper towels to drain. Store in an airtight container in refrigerator. Give with serving instructions.

To serve, preheat oven to 350 degrees. Bake uncovered 5 to 8 minutes or until heated through. Serve with Black-Eyed Pea Soup.

Yield: about 1½ dozen Johnny cakes

''HOMEMADE'' BOX

You will need a wooden box with area suitable for design (we used a 12″ x 6″ x 6″ box), desired color acrylic paint, foam brush, fabric scraps for letters and hearts, coordinating colored paper, paper-backed fusible web, tracing paper, and craft glue.

1. Apply 2 coats of paint to box, allowing to dry between coats.
2. Trace letter and heart patterns onto tracing paper; cut out.
3. For letters, cut a piece of web slightly smaller than each fabric scrap. Follow manufacturer's instructions to fuse web to wrong side of each scrap.
4. Draw around letter patterns on paper side of fabric scraps, spelling ''HOMEMADE'' with letters; cut out letters.
5. Leaving at least ½″ between letters, follow manufacturer's instructions to fuse letters to coordinating paper. Leaving approximately ⅛″ of paper around each letter, cut out letters.
6. For hearts, use heart patterns and cut desired number of hearts from remaining fabric scraps.
7. Arrange letters and hearts on side of box, allowing letters and hearts to overlap if necessary. Glue in place. Allow to dry.

The whole worth of a kind deed lies in the love that inspires it.

— THE TALMUD

What better way to brighten someone's day than with a batch of homemade cookies nestled in this pretty bread cloth! The sweet, nutty taste of Caramel-Macadamia Nut Cookies will provide a friend with delicious proof of your devotion. The simple cloth will serve as a lasting reminder of your kindness.

Preheat oven to 350 degrees. Spread macadamia nuts evenly on an ungreased baking sheet. Stirring occasionally, bake 10 to 15 minutes or until nuts begin to brown. Remove from oven; cool to room temperature.

In a large bowl, cream butter and sugar until fluffy. Add next 3 ingredients; stir until smooth. Add flour; stir until well blended. Fold in macadamia nuts. Drop tablespoonfuls 2 inches apart onto a greased baking sheet. Bake 10 to 12 minutes or until golden brown. Transfer to a wire rack to cool completely. Store in an airtight container.

Yield: about 3 dozen cookies

BREAD CLOTH

You will need a Charles Craft® Ivory Royal Classic bread cover (14 ct) and embroidery floss (see color key).

With outer edges of design 6 fabric threads from beginning of fringe, work design in 1 corner of bread cloth using 2 strands of floss for Cross Stitch and 1 for Backstitch.

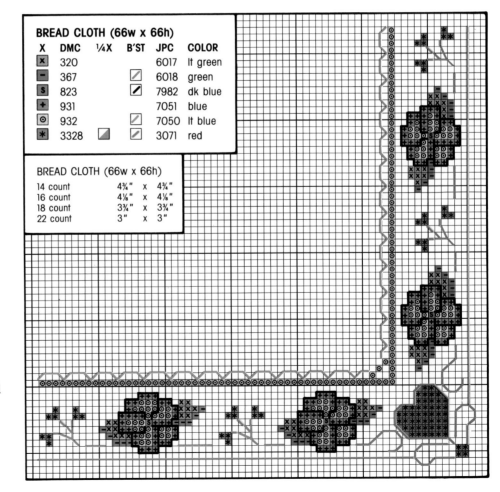

BREAD CLOTH (66w x 66h)

X	DMC	¼X	B'ST	JPC	COLOR
x	320			6017	lt green
-	367		╱	6018	green
S	823		╱	7982	dk blue
+	931			7051	blue
⊙	932		╱	7050	lt blue
✳	3328	◸	╱	3071	red

BREAD CLOTH (66w x 66h)

14 count	4¾"	x	4¾"
16 count	4⅛"	x	4⅛"
18 count	3¾"	x	3¾"
22 count	3"	x	3"

CARAMEL-MACADAMIA NUT COOKIES

1½ cups macadamia nuts, coarsely chopped
1 cup butter or margarine, softened
¾ cup firmly packed brown sugar
1 egg
1 tablespoon corn syrup
1 teaspoon vanilla extract
2 cups all-purpose flour

You're the apple of my eye.

A cherished friend who holds a special place in your eyes will be delighted to receive this yummy Apple-Nut Tart. Almonds play a double role in the delicacy, with a generous sprinkling of slivers on top and a good measure of ground nuts baked in the flaky shell. For country charm, nestle the pie in our dried apple wreath — it will make a homey wall decoration later.

APPLE-NUT TART

CRUST

⅓ cup butter or margarine, softened
½ cup granulated sugar
1 egg
½ teaspoon vanilla extract
1 cup all-purpose flour
⅓ cup finely ground almonds

FILLING

¼ cup half and half
1 tablespoon cornstarch
1 can (21 ounces) apple pie filling
½ teaspoon ground cinnamon

TOPPING

½ cup slivered almonds
1 tablespoon granulated sugar
½ teaspoon ground cinnamon

Preheat oven to 350 degrees. For crust, cream butter and sugar in a large bowl until fluffy. Beat in egg and vanilla. Add flour and almonds; stir until a soft dough forms. Press into bottom and up sides of a greased 11-inch tart pan. Prick with a fork. Bake 10 minutes. Cool completely on a wire rack.

For filling, stir half and half and cornstarch together in a small bowl until smooth. In a small saucepan, combine pie filling and cinnamon. Cook over medium heat, stirring until heated through. Add half and half mixture to pie filling, stirring constantly until mixture begins to boil and thickens. Pour into crust.

For topping, combine all ingredients in a small bowl. Sprinkle evenly over filling. Bake 20 to 25 minutes or until crust is golden brown. Remove from pan and cool completely on a wire rack. Store in an airtight container.

Yield: 8 to 10 servings

APPLE WREATH

You will need an approx. 13″ dia. grapevine wreath, large red apples, paring knife, lemon juice, salt, paper towels, matte clear acrylic spray, 1½″ x 12″ torn fabric strips for bows, almonds (in the shell), desired dried or preserved natural materials (we used dried barley, dried chenopodium, preserved springerii fern, and preserved boxwood), hot glue gun, and glue sticks.

1. (*Note:* We used apple slices that contained a part of the core; each apple will yield only 3 or 4 of these slices.) For dried apple slices, cut ¼″ thick slices from each apple as shown in Fig. 1.

Fig. 1

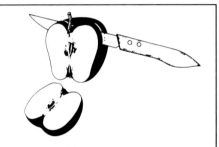

2. Making sure apple slices are completely covered, soak slices for 20 minutes in a mixture of 2 cups of lemon juice and 3 tablespoons of salt. Remove slices from mixture and blot with paper towels to remove excess moisture. Place slices on wire cake racks. Bake at 150 degrees for approximately 6 hours, turning slices over if edges begin to curl. When dried, slices should be pliable and have a leathery feel.

3. Apply 2 coats of acrylic spray to apple slices, allowing to dry between coats.

4. Tie fabric strips into bows.

5. Arrange dried or preserved materials, bows, almonds, and apple slices on wreath; glue to secure.

A cheerful friend is like a sunny day, which sheds its brightness on all around.

— SIR JOHN LUBBOCK

A friend who always brightens your day will be thrilled to receive this cheerful gift. Alternating layers of orange- and lemon-flavored gelatin give these fruity Sunshine Parfaits an inviting appearance. Delivered in a cute cardboard carrier decorated with a beaming sun and puffy white clouds, the refreshing treats are sure to please. Your friend can continue to enjoy the glass tumblers and carton after the desserts are gone.

SUNSHINE PARFAITS

    4 cups water, divided
    1 box (3 ounces) orange-flavored
        gelatin
    1 box (3 ounces) lemon-flavored
        gelatin
    1 cup sour cream, divided
    1 can (11 ounces) mandarin
        oranges, drained
    1 can (8 ounces) pineapple tidbits,
        drained
      Whipped cream and fresh mint
        leaves for garnish (optional)

In a small saucepan, bring 2 cups water to a boil over high heat. Remove from heat. Add orange gelatin; stir until dissolved. Repeat with remaining water and lemon gelatin.

Pour ½ of orange gelatin into a small bowl. Add ½ cup sour cream; stir until well blended. Repeat for lemon gelatin. Add mandarin oranges to remaining orange gelatin. Add pineapple to remaining lemon gelatin. Cover and chill all gelatin mixtures until partially set.

Pour orange-sour cream mixture evenly into 4 tall glasses. Layer mandarin orange mixture, lemon-sour cream mixture, and pineapple mixture evenly into glasses. Cover and refrigerate until set. If desired, garnish with whipped cream and fresh mint leaves before giving gift.

Yield: 4 parfaits

PARFAIT CARRIER

You will need a cardboard carrying carton (we used a bottled water carton), gesso, lt blue and white acrylic paint, foam brushes, small flat paintbrush, tracing paper, orange and yellow paper, and craft glue.

1. Apply 1 coat of gesso and 1 coat of lt blue paint to carton, allowing to dry between coats.
2. Trace patterns onto tracing paper; cut out. Use a pencil to draw around clouds on sides of carton. Paint clouds white. Allow to dry.
3. Use patterns and cut sun and rays from yellow and orange paper. Glue sun to rays. Glue rays to handle of carton. Allow to dry.

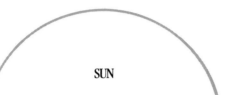

SUN

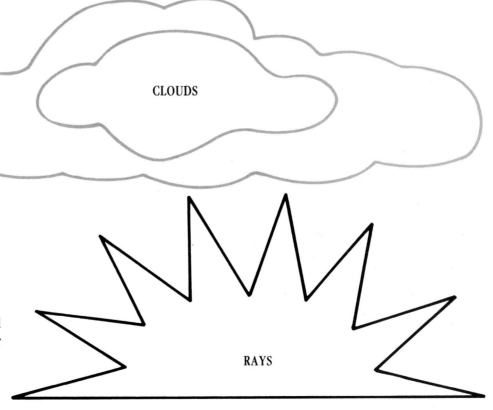

CLOUDS

RAYS

Handsomely trimmed with gold braid, these book boxes look like the real thing! They're perfect for an avid reader who likes to keep a secret cache of goodies nearby. Whether studying for an exam or skimming a best-seller, your friend will enjoy the sweet, nutty flavor of our Hazelnut Chewies.

HAZELNUT CHEWIES

1 cup butter or margarine, softened
⅔ cup firmly packed brown sugar
½ cup granulated sugar
2 tablespoons vegetable oil
1 tablespoon corn syrup
2 eggs
2 teaspoons vanilla extract
2 cups all-purpose flour
¾ teaspoon baking powder
¼ teaspoon salt
1 cup sweetened shredded coconut
1 cup finely chopped hazelnuts

Preheat oven to 350 degrees. In a large bowl, cream butter and sugars until fluffy. Add next 4 ingredients; beat until smooth. In a medium bowl, sift together next 3 ingredients. Add dry ingredients to creamed mixture; stir until a soft dough forms. Fold in coconut and hazelnuts. Drop teaspoonfuls 2 inches apart onto a greased baking sheet. Bake 10 to 12 minutes or until brown. Transfer to a wire rack to cool completely. Store in an airtight container.

Yield: about 7½ dozen cookies

BOOK BOXES

For each box, you will need a pencil box or cigar box, desired color Con-Tact® self-adhesive plastic, medium weight cardboard (mat board), craft knife, desired fabric for cover, desired gold trims, and craft glue.

1. Cover inside and outside of box with self-adhesive plastic.
2. Referring to Fig. 1, measure around box from top front edge to bottom front edge; add 1″ to measurement. Measure length of box; add ¾″ to measurement. Cut cardboard the determined measurements. Cut fabric 1½″ larger on all sides than cardboard.

Fig. 1

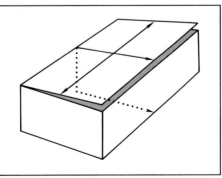

3. Referring to Fig. 2, center back of box on cardboard. Use craft knife to score cardboard along top back edge and bottom back edge of box, extending score lines (indicated by dashed lines) to top and bottom edges of cardboard.

Fig. 2

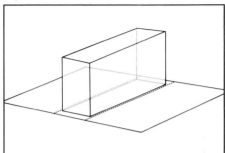

4. To cover cardboard with fabric, center cardboard on fabric with scored side of cardboard facing wrong side of fabric. Glue edges of fabric to top (wrong side) of cardboard; allow to dry. Fold cardboard to wrong side along scored lines.
5. With back of box centered between top and bottom edges of cardboard, place box in folded cardboard. Glue to secure; allow to dry.
6. To decorate book box, cut lengths of trim same width as spine of book box; glue to spine. Cut lengths of trim ¾″ longer than front of book box. With ⅜″ of trim extending at top and bottom edge, glue trim to front; glue ends of trim to wrong side of cover. Allow to dry.

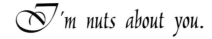

Delivered in our clever container, Amaretto-Cinnamon Nut Mix is a creative way to say, "I'm nuts about you!" The crunchy snack features whole almonds coated with cinnamon, sugar, and almond liqueur. When the last of the treat is gone, the jar can be used to store odds and ends in the workshop.

AMARETTO-CINNAMON NUT MIX

¼ cup butter or margarine
½ cup granulated sugar, divided
½ teaspoon ground cinnamon
2 tablespoons amaretto liqueur
1 cup unsalted whole almonds

Preheat oven to 425 degrees. In a small saucepan, melt butter over medium heat. Stir in ¼ cup sugar and cinnamon. Bring to a boil, stirring constantly until sugar dissolves. Boil sugar mixture 3 minutes longer. Remove from heat. Add liqueur; stir until well blended. Stir in almonds. Spread evenly on a greased baking sheet. Bake 5 to 8 minutes or until dark brown. Roll in remaining sugar; transfer to aluminum foil to cool completely. Store in an airtight container.

Yield: about 1 cup nut mix

"NUTS" JAR

You will need a jar with flat lid, matte Mod Podge® sealer, foam brush, desired fabric and paper, cotton string, black permanent felt-tip pen with fine point, nuts and bolts, masking tape, high gloss clear epoxy coating (we used Aristocrat™ Epoxy Thick Crystal Clear Coating), and a sharp knife.

1. (*Note:* Use Mod Podge® sealer for all gluing.) Using lid as a pattern, cut a circle from fabric. Cut a smaller circle from paper. Use pen to write "I'm Nuts about YOU!" on paper circle. Glue fabric circle, then paper circle, to lid. Glue string around edge of paper circle. Allow to dry.

2. Allowing to dry between coats, apply 2 coats of sealer to top of lid, including edge of fabric.

3. Arrange nuts and bolts on lid; glue in place. Allow to dry.

4. (*Note:* Read all epoxy coating instructions before beginning.) Use tape to mask off all but top of lid. Carefully following manufacturer's instructions, apply coating to lid; allow to dry. Remove masking tape; use knife to scrape any excess coating from side of lid.

$\mathcal{Y}$ou add sweetness to my life.

These fruity sugars make sweet little gifts! Flavored with powdered soft drink mixes, the sugars are a refreshing addition to iced tea, or you can serve them with cereal or fruit for an eye-opening breakfast treat. They can also be substituted for ordinary sugar in favorite recipes. To lend a personal touch to the jars, top them with miniature straw hats decorated in country style. Little hanging tags make cute labels.

STRAWBERRY-BANANA SUGAR

2 cups granulated sugar
1 package (0.20 ounces) Wyler's® unsweetened Strawberry Split Punch soft drink mix

In a small bowl, combine sugar and drink mix; stir until well blended. Store in an airtight container.

Sprinkle sugar over cereal or fresh fruit, or stir into tea. Flavored sugar may also be substituted for granulated sugar in baking. Include serving suggestions with gift.

Yield: about 2 cups sugar

LEMON SUGAR

2 cups granulated sugar
1 package (0.31 ounces) unsweetened lemonade-flavored soft drink mix

In a small bowl, combine sugar and drink mix; stir until well blended. Store in an airtight container.

Sprinkle sugar over cereal or fresh fruit, or stir into tea. Flavored sugar may also be substituted for granulated sugar in baking. Include serving suggestions with gift.

Yield: about 2 cups sugar

For each straw hat jar topper, hot glue 1 or more lengths of desired ribbon around crown of a 4½" dia. straw doll hat. Tie 1 or more lengths of ribbon into a bow; hot glue bow to hat over ends of ribbon on crown. Hot glue artificial leaves and flowers or leaves and miniature fruit to hat. Use a red pen to write ''Lemon Sugar'' or ''Strawberry-Banana Sugar'' on a purchased tag; hang tag from fruit or flower on hat. Place hat on jar.

*A good neighbor, like an apron,
is comfortable, protecting, and always appreciated a lot.*
— CLAUDIA ROHLING

This friendly gift is a sweet way to show a good neighbor how much you appreciate her. Packed with chopped pecans and dusted with confectioners sugar, moist Blackberry Cupcakes have a wonderful fruity flavor. To accompany the cupcakes, send along an apron adorned with blackberry vines. A gift tag bearing the neighborly quotation would make a nice finishing touch.

BLACKBERRY CUPCAKES

   1 cup butter or margarine, softened
   ¾ cup granulated sugar
   2 eggs
   1 cup blackberry jam
   ¾ teaspoon vanilla extract
  1¾ cups all-purpose flour
   ⅛ teaspoon salt
   ½ cup whipping cream
   1 cup chopped pecans
   Confectioners sugar

Preheat oven to 350 degrees. In a large bowl, cream butter and granulated sugar until fluffy. Add eggs 1 at a time, beating well after each addition. Beat in jam and vanilla. In a medium bowl, sift together flour and salt. Add dry ingredients alternately with whipping cream to creamed mixture; stir until well blended. Fold in pecans. Spoon batter into paper-lined muffin tins, filling each tin ⅔ full. Bake 30 to 35 minutes or until a toothpick inserted in center comes out clean. Transfer to a wire rack to cool completely. Dust with confectioners sugar. Store in an airtight container.

Yield: about 2 dozen cupcakes

BLACKBERRY APRON

You will need a cotton or cotton-blend apron with bib; a cellulose sponge; tracing paper; lt purple, burgundy, dk purple, lt green, green, and dk green fabric paint; foam brushes; green, brown, and black permanent felt-tip pens with fine points; fabric for cummerbund; ¼"w grosgrain ribbon to match apron; and thread to match cummerbund fabric and ribbon.

1. Wash, dry, and press apron.
2. Trace berry and leaf patterns onto tracing paper; cut out.
3. Use patterns and cut 1 berry and 1 leaf from sponge.
4. For berries, wet berry sponge; squeeze out excess water. Use foam brush to apply dk purple paint to sponge. Reapplying paint after each stamp, stamp berries on apron as desired. Allow to dry.
5. For highlights and shadows on berries, repeat Step 4, applying lt purple and burgundy paint to opposite ends of berry sponge and stamping over berries on apron. Allow to dry.
6. For leaves, use green paint and repeat Step 4 with leaf sponge.
7. For highlights and shadows on leaves, use lt green and dk green paint and repeat Step 5 with leaf sponge.
8. Follow paint manufacturer's instructions to heat-set design if necessary.
9. Use black pen to draw scalloped outline around each berry. Use green pen to outline each leaf, to draw small leaves on berries, and to draw vines. Use brown pen to draw tendrils and veins on leaves.
10. For cummerbund, measure width of bib at waistband; cut a piece of fabric 10" wide by the determined measurement. Mark each 10" long edge with a pin.
11. Matching right sides and unmarked edges, fold fabric in half. Using a ½" seam allowance, sew unmarked edges together; press seam open. Turn cummerbund right side out. With seam at center back, press cummerbund flat.
12. Hand baste ¼" and ⅛" from each end of cummerbund. Pull basting threads, drawing up gathers to fit width of apron waistband. Knot basting threads and trim ends.
13. Add 1" to width of apron waistband. Cut 2 lengths of ribbon the determined measurement. Press ends of each length ½" to 1 side (wrong side).
14. To attach cummerbund to apron, center cummerbund on waistband and pin in place. With wrong side down, place 1 ribbon length over each end of cummerbund, covering raw edges; baste in place. Machine stitch along center of each ribbon length to secure. Remove any visible basting threads.
15. Wash apron according to paint manufacturer's instructions.

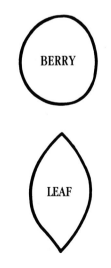

BERRY

LEAF

When friends meet, hearts warm.

With its combination of fresh ingredients, our Spicy Vegetable Salsa will warm up any meeting among friends. A variety of seasonings and vegetables gives the chunky sauce its mild zesty flavor. To accompany the salsa and chips, round up a set of napkins and napkin rings featuring a Southwestern look. A lariat bow and a mini cowboy hat are fun finishing touches for the gift basket.

SPICY VEGETABLE SALSA

½ cup spicy vegetable juice
1 tablespoon lime juice
1 tablespoon lemon juice
1 tablespoon orange juice
1 tablespoon red wine vinegar
2 teaspoons ground dried basil
   leaves
½ teaspoon ground cumin
½ teaspoon ground black pepper
¼ teaspoon hot pepper sauce
¼ teaspoon salt
1 clove garlic, minced

2 tablespoons minced sweet red
   pepper
2 tablespoons minced green pepper
2 tablespoons minced sweet yellow
   pepper
2 tablespoons minced unpeeled
   cucumber
2 tablespoons minced red onion
2 tablespoons minced fresh cilantro

In a medium bowl, combine first 11 ingredients; stir until well blended. Stir in remaining ingredients. Cover and refrigerate 8 hours or overnight to allow flavors to blend. Serve with meat or chips. Include serving suggestions with gift.

Yield: about 1 cup salsa

$\mathcal{A}$ friend is the hope of the heart.

A cherished friend will be charmed by this heartfelt reminder of the close bond you share. Baked in the shape of a heart, our delectable Orange-Chocolate Chiffon Cake is light and airy. A rich dark chocolate glaze enhances the delicate flavor of the cake, while orange peel rosettes make a pretty (and fragrant!) accent. To add a sentimental finishing touch, deliver the dainty dessert in a heart-shaped basket.

ORANGE-CHOCOLATE CHIFFON CAKE

CAKE
- 1 cup all-purpose flour
- ⅔ cup granulated sugar
- 1½ teaspoons baking powder
- ¼ teaspoon salt
- 2 eggs, separated
- ½ cup milk
- ¼ cup vegetable oil
- 2 tablespoons frozen orange juice concentrate, thawed
- 1 teaspoon dried grated orange peel
- 1 teaspoon vanilla extract
- ¼ teaspoon cream of tartar

GLAZE
- 2 ounces unsweetened chocolate
- 2 tablespoons butter or margarine

- 1½ cups confectioners sugar
- 1 teaspoon vanilla extract
- 3 tablespoons plus 1 teaspoon hot water
- 2 oranges for garnish

Preheat oven to 350 degrees. For cake, sift together first 4 ingredients in a large bowl. Add egg yolks and next 5 ingredients. Beat until well blended using medium speed of an electric mixer; set aside.

In another large bowl, beat egg whites until foamy. Add cream of tartar and beat until stiff peaks form. Gently fold egg white mixture into egg yolk mixture. Pour into a greased and floured 8-inch heart-shaped pan. Bake 25 to 30 minutes or until a toothpick inserted in center of cake comes out clean. Leaving cake in pan, turn cake upside down on a wire rack to cool completely. Using cake pan as a pattern, cut a heart-shaped piece of cardboard. Place cooled cake on cardboard.

For glaze, melt chocolate and butter in a small saucepan over low heat; stir until smooth. Remove from heat; add sugar and vanilla. Stir until crumbly. Add water and stir until smooth. Spread glaze on sides and top of cake.

For garnish, cut one ⅛ x 4-inch strip of orange peel. Tie into a bow; set aside. For roses, remove remaining peel from oranges in 1-inch wide strips. Roll 1 strip of peel into a cone shape, then surround with another strip. Continue with remaining strips of peel until rose is desired size. Secure with toothpick. Repeat for remaining 2 roses. Arrange roses and bow on cake. Cover until ready to present.

Yield: about 10 servings

Presented in a handcrafted treasure chest, Strawberry Gem Cookies are a delectable way to show someone that you value her friendship. The cookies, featuring coconut and pistachios, are dusted with confectioners sugar and topped with sparkling jam. When the cookies have been eaten, the richly decorated gift box can be used to hold jewelry.

STRAWBERRY GEM COOKIES

- 1 cup butter or margarine, softened
- ¼ cup granulated sugar
- 2 tablespoons water
- 1 teaspoon vanilla extract
- 2 cups all-purpose flour
- ¼ teaspoon salt
- 2 cups unsweetened shredded coconut
- ½ cup red shelled pistachios, finely chopped
  Confectioners sugar
- ½ cup strawberry jam

Preheat oven to 350 degrees. In a large bowl, cream butter and sugar until fluffy. Stir in water and vanilla. In a medium bowl, sift together flour and salt. Gradually add flour mixture to creamed mixture; stir until a soft dough forms. Fold in coconut and pistachios. Shape dough into 1-inch balls and place 2 inches apart on a greased baking sheet. Using the end of a wooden spoon, make a depression in the center of each cookie. Bake 15 to 20 minutes or until light brown. Transfer to a wire rack. Dust warm cookies with confectioners sugar. Spoon about ½ teaspoon jam into center of each cookie. Allow to cool completely. Store in an airtight container.

Yield: about 3 dozen cookies

JEWELRY BOX

You will need a wooden box with lid (we used a 7¼″ x 5″ x 3¼″ box), glossy black spray paint, fabric to cover lid, gold gimp trim (we used ½″w trim around edge of lid and ¾″w trim for box lid ornament), 1 faux jewel, 1 tassel, and craft glue.

1. Spray paint box and lid black; allow to dry.
2. To cover lid, refer to Fig. 1 and measure length and width of lid including sides; add 1″ to length measurement. Cut fabric the determined measurements.

Fig. 1

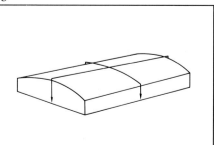

3. Center top of lid on wrong side of fabric piece. Referring to Fig. 2 and matching long raw edges of fabric to long bottom edges of lid, glue fabric to lid. Allow to dry.

Fig. 2

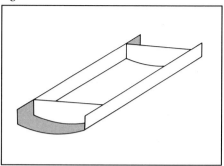

4. Fold 1 short edge of fabric as shown in Fig. 3; glue to side of lid to secure. Repeat for remaining short edge. Allow to dry. Trim excess fabric even with bottom edge of lid.

Fig. 3

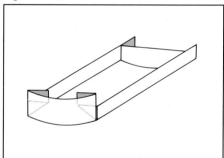

5. Glue gimp trim around bottom edge of lid, covering raw edges of fabric.
6. For ornament, form a length of gimp trim into a circle; glue to secure. Glue faux jewel to center front of gimp circle; glue hanging string of tassel to back of circle. Glue ornament to center front of lid. Allow to dry.

A friend who's musically inclined will enjoy these *Treble Clef Meringue Cookies.* Flavored with chocolate and cinnamon, the crispy treats are so light they'll melt in your mouth! For a lyrical presentation, decorate the gift box with a piece of antique sheet music. Finding just the right piece to express your sentiments will make it extra nice.

TREBLE CLEF MERINGUE COOKIES

    2 ounces unsweetened chocolate
    ½ teaspoon ground cinnamon
    1½ cups sifted confectioners sugar, divided
    4 egg whites
    ½ teaspoon cream of tartar

In a blender or food processor fitted with a steel blade, process chocolate, cinnamon, and 1 cup sugar until finely ground. Cover and set aside in a cool place.

In a large bowl, beat egg whites until foamy. Add cream of tartar and remaining sugar; continue to beat until very stiff. Gently fold chocolate mixture into egg white mixture.

Trace pattern onto tracing paper. Cover baking sheets with waxed paper. Spoon meringue mixture into a pastry bag fitted with a large star tip. For each cookie, place pattern under waxed paper and use as a guide to pipe meringue mixture onto waxed paper. Allow cookies to set at room temperature 30 minutes.

Preheat oven to 200 degrees. Bake 2 hours. Cool completely on waxed paper. Carefully peel away waxed paper. Store in an airtight container.

Yield: about 2½ dozen cookies

MUSIC GIFT BOX

You will need a front cover cut from an old piece of sheet music (we found ours at an antique store), box with lid at least as large as sheet music cover, colored paper to coordinate with sheet music cover, ribbon same width as side of box lid, transparent tape, and craft glue.

1. Follow Steps 1 - 3 of Gift Box 1 instructions, page 123, to cover box lid with paper.
2. Glue sheet music cover to center top of lid.
3. Cut ribbon 1″ longer than circumference of lid. Glue ribbon to side of lid.

*Then come the wild weather, come sleet or snow,
We will stand by each other however it blow.*

— SIMON DACH

When the blustery winds of winter blow, there's nothing better than sitting down to a good, hot meal of simple fare. Nourishing Stroganoff Stew is filled with chunks of beef, potatoes, carrots, and mushrooms in a rich sour cream gravy. Served with a loaf of fresh bread, it's a satisfying lunch or dinner. To make reheating easy, deliver the stew in a large stockpot for your friend to keep. We chose a handsome blue one.

STROGANOFF STEW

¼ cup all-purpose flour
1 teaspoon salt
½ teaspoon ground black pepper
1⅓ pounds stew meat
1 tablespoon vegetable oil
2 cans (10½ ounces each) beef broth
1½ cups water
2 large potatoes, peeled and chopped
6 carrots, peeled and chopped
1 pound fresh mushrooms, sliced
2 teaspoons dried minced garlic
1 cup sour cream

Sprinkle flour, salt, and pepper evenly over meat. In a large stockpot, heat oil over medium heat. Add meat; cook until brown, stirring occasionally. Stirring constantly, gradually add beef broth and water. Add next 4 ingredients. Bring to a boil, reduce heat to medium-low, and simmer 50 to 55 minutes or until potatoes are tender.

Remove from heat; stir in sour cream. Store in an airtight container in refrigerator. Give with serving instructions.

To serve, transfer stew to a large stockpot. Stirring occasionally, cook over medium heat 15 to 20 minutes or until heated through.

Yield: 8 to 10 servings

You're a great catch.

HOOKED
ON
YOU

Flattering a favorite pal is fun with this alluring friendship gift! Simple patterns and food coloring transform our blackberry-flavored cookies into bright "fishing lures." A plain sack rigged up with fishnet, string, and a float makes a captivating carrier for the colorful treats. What a creative way to say, "I'm booked on you"!

FISHING LURE COOKIES

- 1 cup butter or margarine, softened
- ⅓ cup butter-flavored shortening
- ⅓ cup vegetable oil
- 2 cups granulated sugar
- 2 eggs
- 1 teaspoon vanilla extract
- 1 cup blackberry jam
- 6½ cups all-purpose flour
- ½ teaspoon salt
- 3 cups water
  Red, green, yellow, purple, orange, blue, and black paste food coloring

Preheat oven to 350 degrees. In a large bowl, cream first 4 ingredients until fluffy. Add eggs and vanilla; beat until smooth. Stir in jam. In another large bowl, sift together flour and salt.

Add dry ingredients to creamed mixture; knead until a soft dough forms.

For fishing lure patterns, follow Transferring Patterns, page 122. On a lightly floured surface, use a floured rolling pin to roll out dough to ¼-inch thickness. Place patterns on dough and use a sharp knife to cut out cookies. Transfer to a greased baking sheet. Bake 10 to 12 minutes or until golden brown. Transfer to a wire rack to cool completely.

Pour ½ cup water in each of 6 small bowls. Add a small amount of red food coloring to 1 bowl; stir until dissolved. Repeat for all colors except black. To decorate cookies, use a small round paintbrush to lightly brush diluted food coloring onto cookies to resemble fishing lures. Referring to photo, use a small round paintbrush and undiluted black food coloring to paint eyes on cookies. Allow to dry. Store in an airtight container.

Yield: about 6 dozen cookies

FISHY GIFT BAG

You will need a lunch-size paper bag, an approx. 6" x 30" piece of fishnet (available at craft stores), a cork float, hot glue gun, glue sticks, tracing paper, paper for hook, paper for tag, felt-tip pen, hole punch, and cotton string.

1. Fold top of bag 1" to outside; fold 1" to outside again.
2. Gathering ends together, wrap net around bag, overlapping ends at 1 front edge of bag; glue in place.
3. Glue cork float over overlapped area of net.
4. Trace hook pattern onto tracing paper; cut out. Use hook pattern and cut hook from hook paper. Cut tag shape from tag paper. Punch holes in hook and tag.
5. Use pen to write "HOOKED ON YOU" on tag.
6. To secure hook and tag to net, loosely loop and tie string through net and holes in hook and tag.

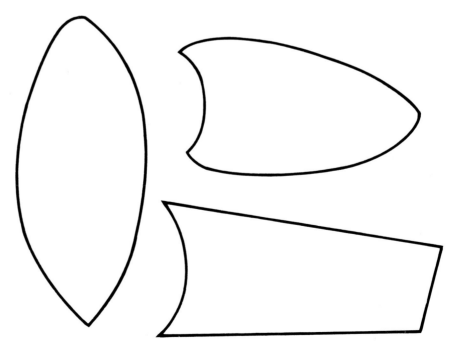

A jar of zesty Blueberry Relish is a cute way to tell a friend that you enjoy her companionship. Packed with blueberries, apples, nuts, and spices, the condiment has a sweet-tart flavor that's great with breads and meat. Our little cross-stitched tote is just the right size for holding a pint of the relish.

BLUEBERRY RELISH

1 bag (16 ounces) frozen unsweetened blueberries, thawed and drained well
1 apple, peeled, cored, and coarsely chopped
1 cup finely chopped pecans
½ cup granulated sugar
2 teaspoons apple cider vinegar
1 teaspoon ground allspice
½ teaspoon ground cinnamon
4 teaspoons lemon juice

In a large saucepan, combine first 7 ingredients. Stirring constantly, bring to a boil over medium heat. Remove from heat. Add lemon juice; stir until well blended. Following Sealing Jars instructions, page 120, fill jar. Store in refrigerator. Serve with meat or bread. Include serving suggestions with gift.

Yield: about 1 pint relish

BLUEBERRY TOTE

You will need 1 Rustico (14 ct) Janlynn® Personal-Wares® Lil' Tote, embroidery floss (see color key), fabric for jar lid insert, craft batting, lightweight cardboard, craft glue, 20″ lengths of desired ribbon, and a small bundle of dried flowers and greenery.

1. Work design on tote using 2 strands of floss for Cross Stitch and 1 for Backstitch.
2. For jar lid insert, follow Jar Lid Finishing, page 122.

3. Tie ribbon lengths together into a bow around jar lid. Tuck bundle of flowers and greenery under ribbon behind bow.

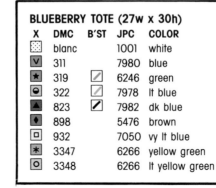

BLUEBERRY TOTE (27w x 30h)

X	DMC	B'ST	JPC	COLOR
⊡	blanc		1001	white
V	311		7980	blue
★	319	╱	6246	green
◉	322	╱	7978	lt blue
▲	823	╱	7982	dk blue
◆	898		5476	brown
▣	932		7050	vy lt blue
✳	3347		6266	yellow green
○	3348		6266	lt yellow green

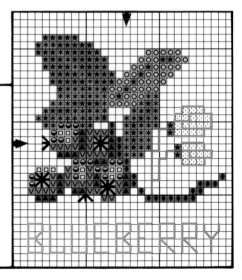

$\mathscr{F}$riendship is the shadow of the evening, which strengthens with the setting sun of life.

— JEAN DE LA FONTAINE

Like twilight's deepening shadows, friendships grow stronger as time goes by. A perfect ending to an evening spent with an old friend, this gift basket features a crock of Nightcap Coffee Mix. Along with the spiced mix, you'll want to add a ceramic mug topped with a whimsical "sleeping cap." It's made from a patterned sock, so why not tuck its mate in, too — the socks will keep your friend's toes toasty while he or she is enjoying the coffee.

NIGHTCAP COFFEE MIX

⅔ cup nondairy powdered coffee
    creamer
⅓ cup instant coffee granules
⅓ cup granulated sugar
1 teaspoon ground cardamom
½ teaspoon ground cinnamon

Combine all ingredients in a medium bowl; stir until well blended. Store in an airtight container. Give with serving instructions.

To serve, spoon 1 heaping tablespoon coffee mix into 8 ounces hot water. Stir until well blended.

Yield: about 1⅓ cups coffee mix

NIGHTCAP BASKET

You will need desired basket; a square of fabric to line basket; a mug; 1 pair of crew-style socks; a cotton ball or small piece of polyester fiberfill; 10" of ¹⁄₁₆"w satin ribbon; 10" of ¹⁄₁₆" dia. metallic cord; and white paper, fabric, felt-tip pen with fine point, and craft glue for label.

1. For cap, place cotton ball in toe of 1 sock. Tie ribbon and cord together into a bow around sock just above cotton ball. Folding cuff to inside of sock, fold cuff in half; folding cuff to outside of sock, fold in half again. Place remaining sock in mug. Place cap over mug.
2. For label on coffee mix container, use pen to write "Nightcap Coffee Mix" on white paper. Cut label desired size. Glue fabric to another piece of paper; glue label to center of fabric-covered paper. Trim fabric-covered paper to ¼" larger than label. Glue label to container.
3. Line basket with fabric square. Place container and mug in basket.

When you share these cute *Watermelon Cookies* with a friend, you're sure to receive a smile in return! Food coloring transforms the sweet treats into miniature watermelon "slices," complete with icing "seeds." Our easy-to-make serving plate, painted with the distinctive markings of a big round watermelon, is the perfect way to present the cookies. What a fun summertime gift!

WATERMELON COOKIES

5 cups all-purpose flour
2 teaspoons baking powder
½ teaspoon salt
1 cup butter or margarine, softened
⅓ cup vegetable oil
⅓ cup butter-flavored shortening
2 cups granulated sugar
2 eggs
1 teaspoon lemon extract
2 teaspoons grated dried lemon peel
  Green and red paste food coloring
1 egg white, lightly beaten
  Purchased white decorating icing
  Black paste food coloring

In a large bowl, sift together first 3 ingredients. In another large bowl, cream next 4 ingredients until fluffy. Add next 3 ingredients; beat until smooth. Transfer 1⅓ cups creamed mixture to a medium bowl; tint green. Tint remaining creamed mixture red. Add 1⅔ cups flour mixture to green mixture; knead until a soft dough forms. Shape dough into a ball, cover, and refrigerate 1 hour. Add remaining flour mixture to red mixture; knead until a soft dough forms. Shape into an 18-inch long log shape; flatten log shape on 1 side. Cover and refrigerate 1 hour.

On a lightly floured surface, use a floured rolling pin to roll out green dough to a 3 x 18-inch rectangle. Brush curved side of red dough with egg white. Wrap green dough around curved side of red dough, trimming if necessary to fit. Cover and refrigerate 1 hour.

Preheat oven to 350 degrees. Slice dough into ¼-inch thick slices. Bake on a greased baking sheet 10 to 12 minutes. Transfer to a wire rack to cool completely.

Transfer icing to a small bowl; tint black. Using a pastry bag fitted with a small round tip, pipe icing onto cookies to resemble seeds. Allow icing to harden. Store in an airtight container.

Yield: about 5½ dozen cookies

WATERMELON PLATE

You will need a wooden plate (available at craft stores); lt yellow green, yellow green, green, and dk green acrylic paint; foam brush; small pieces of cellulose sponge; and clear polyurethane spray.

Note: Plate is for decorative use and should only be used for dry foods. Wipe clean with a damp cloth.

1. Apply 2 coats of lt yellow green paint to plate, allowing to dry between coats.
2. Dip 1 sponge piece in water; squeeze to remove excess. Use sponge piece to lightly stamp entire plate with yellow green paint, allowing lt yellow green to show through. Allow to dry.
3. Dip another sponge piece in water; squeeze to remove excess. Beginning at center of plate and using green paint, use sponge piece to stamp stripes on plate to resemble the end of a watermelon. Allow to dry.
4. Repeat Step 3 using edge of sponge piece and dk green paint to paint narrow dk green stripes over green stripes. Allow to dry.
5. Allowing to dry between coats, apply 2 coats of polyurethane spray to plate.

"Bee" my honey.

A lucky friend will be abuzz with pleasure over this Orange Honey! The delicately flavored honey is delicious served with breads and cakes or drizzled over ice cream. For a playful presentation, dress up a plain basket with silk flowers and chenille bees. A tag made from a silk leaf proudly proclaims, "Glad to 'bee' your friend!"

ORANGE HONEY

   1 cup honey
1½ teaspoons orange-flavored
       extract

In a small bowl, combine honey and extract; stir until well blended. Store in an airtight container.

Serve with bread, crackers, cake, or ice cream. Flavored honey may be substituted for plain honey in baking. Include serving suggestions with gift.

Yield: about 1 cup honey

BEE BASKET

You will need desired basket (we used a 1-quart till basket), artificial leaves and flowers, grosgrain ribbon same width as rim of basket, 2 purchased 1″ long chenille bees, hot glue gun, glue sticks, black permanent felt-tip pen with fine point, 9″ lengths of ¹⁄₁₆″w black and yellow satin ribbon, fabric for jar lid insert, craft batting, lightweight cardboard, craft glue, and green excelsior.

1. Reserving 1 leaf for tag, arrange leaves and flowers along 1 side of basket with stems inside basket; hot glue to secure. Cut grosgrain ribbon ½″ longer than circumference of basket rim. Hot glue ribbon to rim. Hot glue 1 bee to a flower and 1 to basket handle.
2. For tag, cut stem from reserved leaf. Use pen to write the following on leaf: Glad to "BEE" your friend! Cut a small hole near stem end of leaf. Tie lengths of satin ribbon around basket handle. Thread ribbon ends through hole in leaf. Tie ribbon ends into a bow.
3. For jar lid insert, follow Jar Lid Finishing, page 122. Fill basket with excelsior. Place jar of honey in basket.

$\mathcal{A}$h, so fortunate to have a friend like you.

This gift is a fun way to bring good fortune to a friend! A coating of dark chocolate gives purchased fortune cookies a gourmet look and taste. To deliver the crispy treats, spell out our special message on a take-out carton with letters cut from magazines.

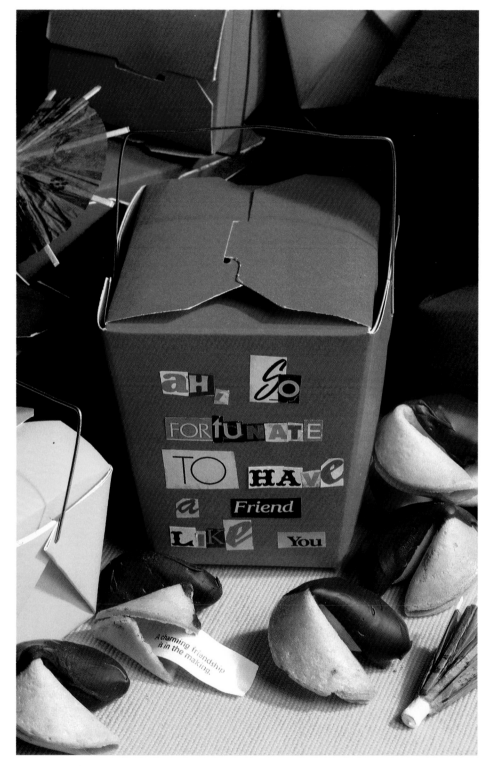

CHOCOLATE-DIPPED FORTUNE COOKIES

1 cup (6 ounces) semisweet
    chocolate chips
1 box (3½ ounces) purchased
    fortune cookies

In a small saucepan, melt chocolate over low heat, stirring constantly. Remove from heat. Dip ½ of each cookie in chocolate. Transfer to a wire rack with waxed paper underneath to cool completely. Store in an airtight container.

Yield: about 1 dozen cookies

For take-out carton, we cut letters from a magazine to spell out ''Ah, so fortunate to have a friend like you'' and used craft glue to glue the letters to 1 side of a purchased Chinese food take-out carton.

Life is to be fortified by many friendships.
— SYDNEY SMITH

Sustaining and supporting us, nutritious foods and nurturing friendships fortify our lives in equally important ways. Our hearty Whole Grain Rye Bread, loaded with healthy ingredients, will be an enriching addition to any meal. A simple cutting board, woodburned with a pretty quilt pattern, will be a lasting reminder of your abiding friendship after the bread is gone.

WHOLE GRAIN RYE BREAD

1½ cups all-purpose flour
1½ cups rye flour
½ cup bran flakes cereal
¼ cup whole wheat flour
1 tablespoon granulated sugar
1 tablespoon caraway seed
1 package active dry yeast
1 teaspoon salt
¼ teaspoon fennel seed
1 ounce unsweetened chocolate
1 cup plus 2 tablespoons water
2 tablespoons molasses
2 tablespoons apple cider vinegar
2 tablespoons butter or margarine
1 teaspoon instant coffee granules

In a large bowl, stir together first 9 ingredients. In a small saucepan, melt chocolate over low heat, stirring constantly. Add remaining ingredients to chocolate and increase heat to medium-low. Stir until mixture reaches

130 degrees (butter may not be completely melted). Stir chocolate mixture into dry ingredients; knead until a soft dough forms.

Turn dough onto a lightly floured surface. Knead about 5 minutes or until dough becomes elastic and pliable. Form into a ball; place in a greased bowl. Grease top of dough and cover. Let rise in a warm place (80 to 85 degrees) 1 hour or until doubled in size. Turn dough onto a lightly floured surface and punch down. Shape dough into a loaf and transfer to a greased 5 x 9-inch baking pan. Grease top of dough and cover. Let rise in a warm place 1 hour or until doubled in size.

Preheat oven to 375 degrees. Bake 35 to 40 minutes or until bread sounds hollow when tapped. Cool completely on a wire rack. Store in an airtight container.

Yield: 1 loaf bread

BREAD BOARD

You will need a wooden cutting board at least 8″ square; tracing paper; graphite transfer paper; woodburning pen; rose, blue, and green liquid fabric dye; paintbrushes; and clear polyurethane spray.

Note: Decorated side of board should not be used for cutting.

1. For quilt block pattern, follow Transferring Patterns, page 122.
2. Use transfer paper to transfer pattern to center of board.
3. Following manufacturer's instructions, use woodburning pen to burn design into board.
4. Diluting dye with water as desired, use dye to paint design, allowing to dry between colors.
5. Allowing to dry between coats, apply 2 coats of polyurethane spray to decorated side of board.

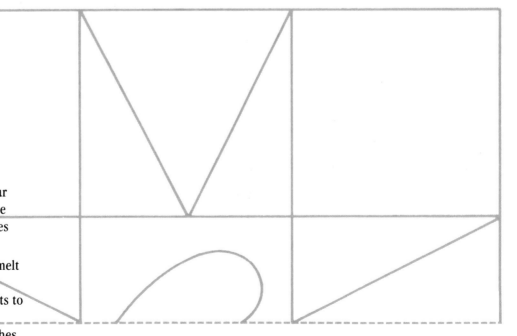

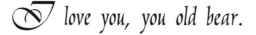 *love you, you old bear.*

To make a big old bear happy, all it takes is a little honey — or our yummy Peanut Butter-Honey Spread! Sure to sweeten a friendship, the cinnamon-spiced spread is great on graham crackers or cookies. For a package that's "un-bear-ably" cute, decorate a bag with our little pom-pom bear and add a heart-shaped tag.

PEANUT BUTTER-HONEY SPREAD

- 1 cup smooth peanut butter
- 1 cup honey
- 1 teaspoon ground cinnamon

Combine all ingredients in a large bowl using medium speed of an electric mixer. Store in an airtight container. Serve with crackers or cookies. Include serving suggestions with gift.

Yield: about 2 cups spread

To decorate jar, cut a piece of batting same size as jar lid; center batting on lid. Center a 6″ dia. fabric circle over batting. Tie a 20″ length of string into a bow around lid to secure fabric. For label, use heart pattern and follow Transferring Patterns, page 122. Use pattern and cut 1 heart from cream-colored paper. Use a felt-tip pen to write "PEANUT BUTTER-HONEY SPREAD" on heart. Glue label to jar.

BEAR BAG

You will need a lunch-size paper bag, five 1″ dia. and one 2″ dia. brown pom-poms, two ¼″ dia. black doll eyes, one ³⁄₁₆″ dia. black bead, 12″ of cotton string, large needle, a 1⅛″w wooden heart cutout (available at craft stores), black felt-tip pen with medium point, scrap of fabric, and craft glue.

1. Place food gift in bag. Fold top of bag 1½″ to back; fold 1½″ to back again.
2. Use needle to make 2 holes through all layers just below center top of bag.

Thread string through holes and tie ends into a bow at front of bag.
3. (*Note:* Allow to dry after each glue step. For head, glue 2″ dia. pom-pom to bag over bow. Glue remaining pom-poms to head and bag for ears, muzzle, and paws. Glue doll eyes to head. Glue bead to muzzle for nose.
4. For heart, write "I Love You" on heart. Glue heart to fabric. Trim fabric to ⅛″ larger than heart. Glue heart to bag below 1 paw.

104

Old and new friends alike will love these two delicious jams! The traditional Grape Jam is perfect for a friend you've held dear for many years, while the innovative Grape-Wine Jam is an ideal offering for a new pal. Bright gold and silver lids and metallic-bordered labels lend a shining touch to the jars. Pretty ribbons and braids woven through a wire basket complete the elegant appearance of the gift.

GRAPE JAM

- 1½ pounds (about 3 cups) red seedless grapes
- 2¼ cups granulated sugar
- 1 cup water
- 1 tablespoon grated dried orange peel
- 1 box (1¾ ounces) pectin

In a large stockpot, combine first 4 ingredients over medium-high heat; stir constantly until sugar dissolves. Bring to a rolling boil. Add pectin; stir until dissolved. Bring to a rolling boil again and boil 1 minute longer. Remove from heat; skim off foam. Following Sealing Jars instructions, page 120, pour into jars. Store in refrigerator.

Yield: about 2 pints jam

GRAPE-WINE JAM

- 1½ pounds (about 3 cups) red seedless grapes
- 2¼ cups granulated sugar
- 1 cup dry red wine
- 1 tablespoon grated dried orange peel
- 1 box (1¾ ounces) pectin

In a large stockpot, combine first 4 ingredients over medium-high heat; stir constantly until sugar dissolves. Bring to a rolling boil. Add pectin; stir until dissolved. Bring to a rolling boil again and boil 1 minute longer. Remove from heat; skim off foam. Following Sealing Jars instructions, page 120, pour into jars. Store in refrigerator.

Yield: about 2 pints jam

JAM BASKET

You will need a wire basket, desired silver and gold cord and ribbon, a purchased bread cloth, silver and gold spray paint, white paper, black felt-tip calligraphy pen with medium point, silver and gold paper, and craft glue.

1. For basket, weave cord and ribbon through basket near rim; tie ends into a bow at front of basket. Knot and trim ends of cord. Place bread cloth in basket.
2. For grape jam, spray paint outside of jar lid gold; for grape-wine jam, paint jar lid silver. Allow to dry.
3. For grape jam label, use pen to write ''Grape Jam'' on white paper. Cut label desired size; cut corners from label. Glue label to gold paper; trim paper to ⅛" from label. Glue label to jar. Using silver paper, repeat for grape-wine jam label.

105

A heart for an old friend, a hand for the new.

A longtime symbol of friendship, the heart-and-hand motif lends an old-fashioned air to these coffee-flavored cookies. Whether presented to an old friend or a new one, a basket of the shortbread treats is a nice way to say, ''Glad we're friends.'' A string of puffy hearts sewn from country print fabrics makes a charming accent.

HEART-AND-HAND COOKIES

1 cup butter or margarine, softened
⅓ cup butter-flavored shortening
⅓ cup vegetable oil
2 cups granulated sugar
2 eggs
1 teaspoon vanilla extract
2 tablespoons instant coffee granules
1 tablespoon hot water
5 cups all-purpose flour
½ teaspoon salt

Preheat oven to 350 degrees. In a large bowl, cream first 4 ingredients until fluffy. Add eggs and vanilla; beat until smooth. In a small bowl, dissolve coffee in water; stir into creamed mixture. In another large bowl, sift together flour and salt. Add dry ingredients to creamed mixture; knead until a soft dough forms.

For cookie pattern, use heart-and-hand pattern and follow Transferring Patterns, page 122. On a lightly floured surface, use a floured rolling pin to roll out dough to ¼-inch thickness. Place pattern on dough and use a sharp knife to cut out cookies. Transfer to a greased baking sheet. Bake 10 to 12 minutes or until golden brown. Transfer to a wire rack to cool completely. Store in an airtight container.

Yield: about 2½ dozen cookies

HEART BASKET

You will need a basket; two 5″ squares of fabric for each heart; thread to match fabrics; polyester fiberfill; buttons; tracing paper; fabric marking pencil; hot glue gun; glue sticks; coordinating cotton yarn; fabric square to line basket; and paper, fabric, craft glue, large needle, and pinking shears for tag.

1. Use heart pattern and follow Transferring Patterns and Sewing Shapes, page 122, to make desired number of hearts. Stuff hearts with fiberfill; sew final closures by hand. Referring to photo, sew 2 buttons to each heart.
2. With hearts approximately ½″ apart, hot glue hearts around basket.
3. Cut 5″ lengths of yarn. Loop 1 length around each button. Knot together yarn ends between hearts; trim ends to 1½″.
4. For tag, write message on paper; use pinking shears to cut tag desired size. Use craft glue to glue fabric to another piece of paper; glue tag to center of fabric-covered paper. Use regular scissors to trim fabric-covered paper to ¼″ larger than tag. Glue buttons to tag. Use needle to thread a length of yarn through 1 corner of tag. Tie yarn into a bow around basket handle.
5. Line basket with fabric square.

HEART

107

No one else can fill your shoes.

Here's a lighthearted way to let a special friend know that no one could take his place in your heart. Inside this memorable, easy-to-decorate shoe box is a loaf of hearty Bacon Batter Bread just brimming with smoky flavor. Add a clever gift tag, and this "loafer" bread is one he won't soon forget!

BACON BATTER BREAD

- 1   pound bacon
- 3   cups all-purpose flour
- ¼   cup granulated sugar
- 2   tablespoons baking powder
- 2   teaspoons salt
- 3   eggs
- ½   teaspoon liquid smoke flavoring
- 1½ cups milk

In a large skillet, cook bacon over medium heat until crisp. Transfer to paper towels to drain; reserve ⅓ cup bacon drippings. Cool bacon to room temperature, crumble, and set aside.

Preheat oven to 350 degrees. In a large bowl, combine next 4 ingredients.

In a medium bowl, whisk together reserved bacon drippings and next 3 ingredients. Add egg mixture to dry ingredients; stir just until moistened. Fold in bacon. Pour batter into a greased 5 x 9-inch loaf pan. Bake 45 to 50 minutes or until a toothpick inserted in center comes out clean. Cool in pan 10 minutes; turn onto a wire rack to cool completely. Store in an airtight container.

Yield: 1 loaf bread

SHOE BOX

You will need a shoe box with lid, wrapping paper, brown craft paper, transparent tape, pictures of shoes cut from catalogs or magazines, paper for tag, a black felt-tip pen, craft glue, waxed paper, and cotton string.

1. Using wrapping paper for lid and craft paper for box, follow Gift Box 1 instructions, page 123.
2. Reserving 1 shoe cutout for tag, arrange shoe cutouts on lid; glue to secure.
3. For tag, use pen to write the following on paper: A "LOAFER" BREAD FOR YOU. Glue reserved shoe cutout close to words. Cut tag desired size and shape.
4. Line box with waxed paper. Place loaf of bread in box. Place lid on box and tie string into a bow around box.

You're one in a million.

Expressing your affection for a one-in-a-million friend is easy with this cleverly decorated Pineapple Cake. Crushed pineapple, chopped walnuts, and sour cream, along with a hint of nutmeg and vanilla, give the moist cake a delicious flavor. The whimsical "paper doll" chain is simple to create with decorating icing. What a nice way to let an extra-special pal know she really stands out in your circle of friends!

PINEAPPLE CAKE

CAKE
- 1¾ cups all-purpose flour
- 1 teaspoon baking powder
- 1 teaspoon baking soda
- 1 teaspoon ground nutmeg
- ½ teaspoon salt
- ¾ cup firmly packed brown sugar
- 1 cup drained, canned crushed pineapple
- ½ cup finely chopped walnuts
- 1 cup sour cream
- ⅓ cup vegetable oil
- 1 egg
- 2 teaspoons vanilla extract

ICING
- 6 cups confectioners sugar
- 6 tablespoons milk
- Black and yellow paste food coloring
- Purchased chocolate-flavored and blue decorating icing

Preheat oven to 350 degrees. For cake, sift together first 5 ingredients in a large bowl. Stir in next 3 ingredients. Add remaining ingredients; blend well using medium speed of an electric mixer. Pour batter into a greased and floured 9 x 13-inch baking pan. Bake 35 to 40 minutes or until a toothpick inserted in center of cake comes out clean. Cool completely on a wire rack.

For icing, combine sugar and milk in a large bowl; beat until smooth. Transfer ½ cup icing to a small bowl; tint black and cover. Transfer another ¼ cup white icing to a small bowl; tint yellow and cover. Spread remaining white icing over top of cake. Allow icing to harden.

To transfer pattern to top of cake, trace doll pattern onto tracing paper. Connecting hands, trace 2 additional dolls. Center entire pattern on cake and use a toothpick to punch holes about ¼-inch apart through pattern into icing. Remove pattern. Transfer black icing to a pastry bag fitted with a very small round tip. Pipe black icing around edges of paper doll design on cake. Pipe black icing on center doll for face, sleeves, legs, and shoes. Spread yellow icing on center doll for dress. Allow icing to harden. Use a small round tip to pipe blue icing on dress for collar and buttons. Transfer chocolate-flavored icing to a pastry bag fitted with a grass tip. Pipe chocolate-flavored icing for hair. Allow icing to harden. Cover with plastic wrap.

Yield: 12 to 14 servings

The ornament of a house is the friends who frequent it.
— RALPH WALDO EMERSON

A warm, welcoming atmosphere makes a home an enjoyable place for friends to visit. To show your appreciation to a family whose door is always open, surprise them with these crispy Ginger-Peanut Butter Cookies. Along with the house-shaped cookies, you'll want to make our hand-painted plaque — it will make a homey ornament for their wall or door.

GINGER-PEANUT BUTTER COOKIES

1 cup butter or margarine, softened
⅓ cup butter-flavored shortening
⅓ cup vegetable oil
2 cups granulated sugar
2 eggs
1 teaspoon vanilla extract
1 cup smooth peanut butter
5 cups all-purpose flour
1 teaspoon ground ginger
½ teaspoon salt

Preheat oven to 350 degrees. In a large bowl, cream first 4 ingredients until fluffy. Add eggs and vanilla; beat until smooth. Stir in peanut butter. In another large bowl, sift together remaining ingredients. Add dry ingredients to creamed mixture; knead until a soft dough forms.

For cookie pattern, use large house pattern (in grey) and follow Transferring Patterns, page 122. On a lightly floured surface, use a floured rolling pin to roll out dough to ¼-inch thickness. Place pattern on dough and use a sharp knife to cut out cookies. Transfer to a greased baking sheet. Bake 10 to 12 minutes or until golden brown. Transfer to a wire rack to cool completely. Store in an airtight container.

Yield: about 6 dozen cookies

WELCOME PLAQUE

You will need a 6″ x 4¼″ *oval wooden plaque, tracing paper, graphite transfer paper, acrylic paint (see color key), Duncan Quik-Crackle™ crackling medium, black permanent felt-tip pen with fine point, waterbase wood stain, matte waterbase varnish, paintbrushes, and a soft cloth.*

1. For basecoat, paint plaque dk brown. Using cream paint for contrast, follow manufacturer's instructions to apply crackling medium and paint to front of plaque; allow to dry.
2. Trace plaque pattern onto tracing paper. Use transfer paper to transfer design to center of plaque.
3. Allowing paint to dry between colors, refer to photo and color key to paint plaque. Use pen to draw over outlines and detail lines.
4. Apply stain to plaque; remove excess with soft cloth. Allow to dry.
5. Apply varnish to plaque. Allow to dry.

COLOR KEY

Basecoat - dk brown
Contrast (front of plaque only) - cream
House - tan
Door - blue
Window - white
Shutters - red
Chimney - dk red
Roof and lettering - dk tan

We have been friends together in sunshine and in shade.

— CAROLINE NORTON

Packed with everything you'll need for a picnic, this hamper is perfect for sharing in a quiet, shady spot. The meal for two includes savory Chicken Turnovers, tropical banana-flavored Sunshine Punch, and purchased cookies for dessert. We lined our hamper with colorful fabric and included plates, glasses, and matching napkins. Your friend will enjoy using it for other outings, too!

SUNSHINE PUNCH

3 bananas, peeled and cut into
   pieces
1 can (6 ounces) frozen lemonade
   concentrate, thawed
4 cups water
2 cups red grape juice
1 can (6 ounces) frozen pineapple
   juice concentrate, thawed

In a blender or food processor fitted with a steel blade, process bananas and lemonade concentrate until well blended. Transfer to a 3-quart container. Add remaining ingredients; stir until well blended. Cover and refrigerate. Serve chilled.

Yield: about 2½ quarts punch

CHICKEN TURNOVERS

1 tablespoon sesame oil
6 green onions, chopped
½ pound fresh mushrooms, chopped
3 cloves garlic, minced
½ teaspoon salt
¼ teaspoon ground black pepper
1 can (5 ounces) chicken, drained
1 package (17¼ ounces) frozen
   puff pastry dough, thawed
   according to package directions
4 ounces Havarti cheese, grated

Preheat oven to 350 degrees. In a large skillet, heat oil over medium heat. Add next 5 ingredients; sauté until onions are brown. Stir in chicken. Remove from heat.

On a lightly floured surface, use a floured rolling pin to roll out each sheet of pastry to an 8 x 12-inch rectangle. Using a sharp knife, cut pastry into 4-inch squares. Spoon about 1 tablespoon chicken mixture into center of each square. Sprinkle about 2 teaspoons cheese over chicken mixture. Fold pastry over chicken and

cheese, forming a triangle. Crimp edges together with a fork. Transfer to a greased baking sheet. Bake 20 to 25 minutes or until brown. Transfer to a wire rack to cool completely. Store in an airtight container in refrigerator. Give with serving instructions.

Turnovers may be served at room temperature or reheated. To reheat, preheat oven to 350 degrees. Bake uncovered on an ungreased baking sheet 8 to 10 minutes or until heated through.

Yield: 1 dozen turnovers

PICNIC SET

For basket, you will need a picnic basket with hinged lid, fabric for lining and ruffle, thread to match fabric, purchased piping to coordinate with fabric, medium weight cardboard, craft batting, fabric marking pencil, hot glue gun, and glue sticks.
For napkins, you will need four 16" squares of fabric, tracing paper, fabric marking pencil, purchased extra-wide double-fold bias tape to coordinate with fabric, and thread to match bias tape.

1. To determine size of lining fabric, measure height of basket and add 2"; measure circumference of basket at widest point and add 1". Cut lining fabric the determined measurements.
2. Cut a length of piping same length as lining fabric. Matching raw edges, baste piping along 1 long edge (top edge) on right side of lining fabric.
3. For ruffle, cut a strip of fabric 3" wide and twice the length of lining fabric. Matching wrong sides, fold strip in half lengthwise; press. Baste ½" and ¼" from raw edge. Pull basting threads, drawing up gathers to fit top edge of lining fabric. Matching right sides and raw edges, baste ruffle to top

edge of lining fabric.
4. Using a zipper foot and sewing as close to piping as possible, sew ruffle and piping to lining fabric. Press seam allowance toward lining fabric.
5. Matching right sides and short edges, fold lining fabric in half. Using a ½" seam allowance, sew short edges together. Press seam allowance open.
6. With top edge of ruffle even with top edge of basket, glue lining to inside of basket along ruffle seamline.
7. For padded bottom liner, draw around bottom of basket on cardboard; cut out cardboard shape ¼" inside drawn line. Place cardboard inside basket and trim to fit if necessary. Follow Making Padded Shapes, page 122, to make liner. Glue liner to inside bottom of basket, covering raw edge of lining.
8. For padded lid liner, draw around basket lid on cardboard; cut out cardboard shape 1" inside drawn line. Follow Making Padded Shapes, page 122, to make liner. Cut a length of piping 1" longer than circumference of liner; glue raw edge of piping to back of liner. Center and glue liner to inside of lid.
9. For napkin pattern, cut a 4" square from tracing paper; round off 1 corner.
10. For each napkin, match rounded corner of pattern to 1 corner of fabric square; use fabric marking pencil to draw around rounded corner of pattern. Repeat for remaining corners of fabric square. Cut along each drawn line.
11. Apply bias tape to edge of each napkin for binding.

Friendship Day, the first Sunday in August, is set aside for remembering those special people who mean so much to us. With our luscious Caramel Fudge recipe and simple bag decorating ideas, you can make sweet little gifts for lots of your friends. We used lunch-size bags, but any size will do. Pretty fabrics add charm to hand-written paper tags.

CARAMEL FUDGE

- 4 cups granulated sugar
- 1 cup evaporated milk
- 1/3 cup light corn syrup
- 6 tablespoons butter or margarine
- 2 tablespoons honey
- 1/2 teaspoon vanilla extract
- 1 cup chopped pecans

Butter sides of a large stockpot. Combine first 5 ingredients in pot and cook over medium-low heat, stirring constantly until sugar dissolves. Using a pastry brush dipped in hot water, wash down any sugar crystals on sides of pot. Attach candy thermometer to pot, making sure thermometer does not touch bottom of pot. Increase heat to medium and bring to a boil. Do not stir while syrup is boiling. Cook until syrup reaches soft ball stage (approximately 234 to 240 degrees). Test about 1/2 teaspoon syrup in ice water. Syrup should easily form a ball in ice water but flatten when held in your hand. Place pot in 2 inches of cold water in sink. Add vanilla; do not stir until syrup cools to approximately 110 degrees.

Using medium speed of an electric mixer, beat fudge until it is no longer glossy and thickens. Pour into a buttered 8 x 11-inch baking dish. Sprinkle pecans evenly on top. Cool completely in pan. Cut into 1-inch squares. Store in an airtight container in refrigerator.

Yield: about 7 dozen pieces fudge

GIFT BAGS

For each bag, you will need 1 approx. 6"w x 11"h gift bag, hole punch, tracing paper, and waxed paper.
For scalloped bag, you will also need 20" of 1½"w ribbon for bow.
For doily bag, you will also need one 6" dia. paper doily, 20" lengths of desired ribbon for bow, a 4" square of clear cellophane, and craft glue.
For each tag, you will need white paper, a felt-tip pen, fabric, craft glue, pinking shears, a large needle, and 9" of 1/16"w ribbon.

SCALLOPED BAG

1. Trim top of bag to 3" taller than desired finished height of bag. Cutting through all layers, cut approximately 1" wide scallops in top edge of bag. Punch 1 hole in center of each scallop.
2. For handle, trace handle pattern onto tracing paper; cut out. Fold top of bag 3" to front. Center fold line of handle pattern (indicated on pattern by dotted line) 1" from top on front of bag; use a pencil to lightly draw around handle pattern. Cutting through all layers along cutting line only (indicated on pattern by solid line), cut out handle.
3. Unfold top of bag. Line bottom of bag

with waxed paper; place fudge in bag.
4. Refold top of bag; fold all layers of handle to back of bag along fold line. Thread ribbon through handle opening and tie ends into a bow; trim streamers.

DOILY BAG

1. For heart "window," trace heart pattern onto tracing paper; cut out. Draw around heart pattern on front of bag. Cutting through front of bag only, cut out heart. Glue cellophane to inside of bag, covering heart-shaped opening. Allow to dry.
2. Line bottom of bag with waxed paper; place fudge in bag.
3. Trim top of bag to 1½" taller than desired finished height of bag. Fold top of bag 1½" to back. Fold doily in half. Place doily over top of bag. Punching through all layers, punch 2 holes 1" apart 1" below center top of bag. Thread ribbon lengths through holes and tie into a bow at front of bag; trim streamers.

TAG

1. Use pen to write name on a piece of white paper. Cut tag desired size.
2. Glue a piece of fabric to another piece of paper. Glue tag to center of fabric-covered paper. Allow to dry.
3. Use pinking shears to trim fabric-covered paper to ¼" larger than tag.
4. Use needle to thread ribbon through 1 corner of tag. Knot ends together. Hang tag around bow on gift bag.

HEART

HANDLE

Friendship is a tapestry woven through the years with threads of joy and laughter, happiness and tears.

As rich and sweet as the tapestry of friendship, these nutty cookies are guaranteed to delight. Brimming with walnuts, raisins, and coconut, their fruity taste is enhanced by a touch of rum flavoring. And they're as easy to make as the showy tasseled bag in which you'll present them. Simply tuck a generous portion of the cookies inside the bag; it can later be used for storing jewelry or as an elegant travel accessory.

RUM-RAISIN BALLS

1½ cups granulated sugar, divided
1 cup chopped walnuts
1 cup sweetened shredded coconut
1 cup raisins
2 eggs, beaten
1 teaspoon rum-flavored extract

Preheat oven to 350 degrees. In a large bowl, combine 1 cup sugar and remaining ingredients; stir until well blended. Spoon into a greased 8-inch square baking dish. Bake 20 to 25 minutes, stirring occasionally. Cool on a wire rack 10 minutes. Using damp hands, shape into 1-inch balls; roll in remaining sugar. Store in an airtight container.

Yield: about 2½ dozen

TAPESTRY GIFT BAG

You will need a 7½" x 23½" piece of fabric, 14½" of ⅞"w trim for top edge of bag, thread to match fabric and trim, 23" of ¹⁄₁₆" dia. gold cord, two ³⁄₁₆" dia. gold beads, a 4" long tassel, and a seam ripper.

1. Follow Steps 2 and 4 of Fabric Bag instructions, page 122; do not turn bag right side out.
2. For casing, press top edge of bag 2" to wrong side. Machine stitch 1¾" and 1½" from pressed edge. Turn bag right side out. Use seam ripper to open casing on outside of bag at 1 side seam. Thread cord through casing. Thread 1 bead onto each end of cord and knot each end.
3. Overlapping ends of trim, machine stitch trim to top edge of bag.
4. Place a plastic bag of cookies in bag. Pull ends of cord to close bag; tie ends into a bow. Hang tassel from bow.

Here's a way to "reward" a friend who adds richness to your life! Quick and easy to make, our Spicy Cheese Snack Mix is a wonderful treat for a favorite pal. A cardboard canister, cleverly covered with play money, makes a lighthearted container for presenting the savory crackers. Your friend's smile will be the priceless payoff you receive in return!

SPICY CHEESE SNACK MIX

1 box (9 ounces) miniature saltine crackers
½ cup butter or margarine
2 packages (1¼ ounces each) cheese sauce mix
½ cup grated Parmesan cheese
½ teaspoon cayenne pepper

Preheat oven to 350 degrees. Pour crackers into a large bowl. In a small saucepan, melt butter over medium heat. Remove from heat; stir in remaining ingredients. Pour over crackers; toss until well coated. Transfer to a baking sheet. Bake 10 to 12 minutes or until light brown. Transfer to paper towels to cool. Store in an airtight container.

Yield: about 4 cups snack mix

MONEY CANISTER

You will need a cardboard canister with resealable lid (we used a 7.5 oz. corn chip canister); play money; matte Mod Podge® sealer; craft knife; gold lamé fabric for lid; craft batting; ¼"w gold gimp trim; 12" of ⅛"w gold braid trim; and paper, black felt-tip pen with fine point, fabric, and 6" of gold metallic thread for tag.

1. (*Note:* Use sealer for all gluing.) Overlapping money and allowing edges to extend beyond top and bottom edges of canister, glue money to side of canister. Allow to dry. Use craft knife to trim money even with top and bottom edges of canister.
2. Apply 2 coats of sealer to side of canister, allowing to dry between coats.
3. To cover lid, use lid as a pattern and cut 1 piece from batting. Draw around lid on wrong side of fabric; cut out fabric circle ½" larger than drawn line. Center batting, then top of lid, on wrong side of fabric circle. At ½" intervals, make cuts into edge of fabric to ⅛" from lid. Pulling fabric taut, glue cut edges of fabric to side of lid, allowing edges of fabric to extend beyond bottom edge of lid. Allow to dry. Trim excess fabric along bottom edge of lid. Glue gimp around side of lid, covering raw edges of fabric. Allow to dry.
4. Tie braid into a bow. Glue bow to side of lid. Allow to dry.
5. For tag, use pen to write "Spicy Cheese Snack Mix" on paper. Cut tag desired size. Glue fabric to another piece of paper; glue tag to center of fabric-covered paper. Trim fabric-covered paper to ¼" larger than tag. Use a needle to thread metallic thread through corner of tag; knot ends together. Hang tag around bow on canister.

117

A friend is one to whom one may pour out the contents
of one's heart, chaff and grain together....

— ARABIAN PROVERB

Sharing your innermost thoughts with someone who understands you is one of the greatest blessings of friendship. Baked for a trusted confidante, a warm loaf of Spaghetti Bread will make a heart-to-heart talk even more enjoyable. Its unique flavor is created with a combination of spaghetti, wheat flour, Parmesan cheese, and zesty Italian seasonings. Given with the bread, a ribbon-tied bouquet of grain will make an elegant, European-style accent for the home.

SPAGHETTI BREAD

3½ ounces (½ of 7-ounce package) thin spaghetti, cooked, drained, and rinsed with cold water
2 cups all-purpose flour
1 cup whole wheat flour
⅓ cup grated Parmesan cheese
1 package active dry yeast
1 tablespoon granulated sugar
1 teaspoon garlic salt
½ teaspoon dried basil leaves
½ teaspoon dried oregano leaves
1½ cups warm water
1 tablespoon olive oil

In a large bowl, combine first 9 ingredients. In a medium bowl, whisk together water and oil. Gradually add oil mixture to dry ingredients; knead until a soft dough forms. Turn dough onto a lightly floured surface and knead about 5 minutes or until dough becomes elastic and pliable. Place dough in a greased bowl; grease top of dough. Cover and let rise in a warm place (80 to 85 degrees) 1 hour or until doubled in size. Turn dough onto a lightly floured surface and punch down. Shape into a loaf and place in a greased 5 x 9-inch loaf pan. Grease top of dough. Cover and let rise in a warm place 1 hour or until doubled in size.

Preheat oven to 350 degrees. Bake 30 to 35 minutes or until brown and bread sounds hollow when tapped. Transfer to a wire rack to cool completely. Store in an airtight container.

Yield: 1 loaf bread

FRENCH GRAIN BOUQUET

You will need desired terra-cotta pot, block of floral foam to fill pot to ½" from top, dried rye (we used approximately 10 dozen stalks), rubber band, paring knife, sheet moss, and 1 yd of ⅞"w wired ribbon.

1. Trim stems of rye stalks to desired length.
2. Bundle rye stalks together; use rubber band to secure.
3. Use knife to cut a hole through center of floral foam approximately the same diameter as rye bundle. Place foam in pot.
4. Insert bundle into hole in foam. Arrange height of rye stalks as desired.
5. Fill pot to rim with moss, covering foam.
6. Tie ribbon into a bow around bundle; trim and arrange streamers as desired.

KITCHEN TIPS

MEASURING INGREDIENTS

Liquid measuring cups have a rim above the measuring line to keep liquid ingredients from spilling. Nested measuring cups (¼, ⅓, ½, and 1 cup) are used to measure dry ingredients, butter, and shortening. Measuring spoons (⅛, ¼, ½, 1 teaspoon, and 1 tablespoon) are used for measuring both dry and liquid ingredients.

To measure flour or granulated sugar: Dip nested measuring cup into ingredient and level top of cup with knife. Do not pack down with spoon.

To measure brown sugar: Pack into nested measuring cup and level top of cup with knife. Sugar should hold its shape when removed from cup.

To measure confectioners sugar: If necessary, sift sugar to remove any lumps. Spoon lightly into nested measuring cup and level top of cup with knife.

To measure shortening or peanut butter: Pack firmly into nested measuring cup and level top of cup with knife.

To measure liquids: Use a liquid measuring cup placed on a flat surface. Pour ingredient into cup and check measuring line at eye level.

To measure honey or syrup: For more accurate measurement, lightly spray measuring cup or spoon with cooking spray before measuring so the liquid will release easily from cup or spoon.

To measure dry ingredients equaling less than ¼ cup: Dip measuring spoon into ingredient and level top of spoon with knife.

TESTS FOR CANDY MAKING

There are 2 ways to determine the correct temperature of cooked candy. The first is to use a candy thermometer. To check the accuracy of a candy thermometer, place it in a small saucepan of water over high heat and bring to a boil. Thermometer should register 212 degrees when water boils. If it does not, adjust the temperature range for each candy consistency accordingly. Insert thermometer into mixture, making sure thermometer does not touch bottom or sides of pan.

The second method to determine the correct temperature of cooked candy is the cold water test. Remove pan from heat and drop about ½ teaspoon of candy mixture into a cup of ice water. Use a fresh cup of water for each test. Use the following descriptions to determine if candy has reached the correct consistency:

Soft Ball Stage (234 to 240 degrees): candy can be rolled into a soft ball in ice water but will flatten when held in your hand.

Firm Ball Stage (242 to 248 degrees): candy can be rolled into a firm ball in ice water but will flatten if pressed when removed from the water.

Hard Ball Stage (250 to 268 degrees): candy can be rolled into a hard ball in ice water and will remain hard when removed from the water.

Soft Crack Stage (270 to 290 degrees): candy will form hard threads in ice water but will soften when removed from the water.

Hard Crack Stage (300 to 310 degrees): candy will form brittle threads in ice water and will remain brittle when removed from the water.

SEALING JARS

To seal jars, wash jars, lids, and screw rings in soapy water; rinse well. Place jars on a rack in a large Dutch oven. Place lids and screw rings in a saucepan; cover jars, lids, and screw rings with water. Bring both pans to a boil; boil 10 minutes. Remove from heat, leaving jars, lids, and screw rings in hot water until ready to use. Immediately before filling, remove jars from hot water and drain well. Fill hot jars to within ¼ inch of tops; wipe jar rims and threads. Quickly cover with lids and screw rings on tightly. Invert jars 5 minutes; turn upright. If food is to be canned, use water-bath method as directed by the USDA. If food is not canned, store in refrigerator.

SOFTENING BUTTER

To soften butter or margarine, remove wrapper from butter and place on a microwave-safe plate. Microwave 1 stick 20 to 30 seconds at medium-low (30%).

SOFTENING CREAM CHEESE

To soften cream cheese, remove wrapper from cream cheese and place on a microwave-safe plate. Microwave 1 to 1½ minutes at medium (50%) for one 8-ounce package or 30 to 45 seconds for one 3-ounce package.

SUBSTITUTING HERBS

To substitute fresh herbs for dried, use 1 tablespoon fresh chopped herbs for ½ teaspoon dried herbs.

BEATING EGG WHITES

For greatest volume, beat egg whites at room temperature in a clean, dry metal or glass bowl.

WHIPPING CREAM

For greatest volume, chill bowl, beaters, and cream 1 hour before whipping. In warm weather, place chilled bowl over ice while whipping cream.

CUTTING COOKIE SHAPES

To cut out cookie shapes, dip cookie or biscuit cutter in water to keep dough from sticking to cutter.

MELTING CHOCOLATE

To melt chocolate, place chopped or shaved chocolate in top of a double boiler (or in a heat-proof bowl over a saucepan of water) over hot, not boiling water. Stir occasionally until melted. Remove from heat and use chocolate for dipping as desired. If necessary, chocolate may be returned to heat to remelt.

GRATING CHEESE

To grate cheese easily, place wrapped cheese in freezer for 10 to 20 minutes before grating.

TOASTING NUTS

To toast nuts, spread nuts evenly on an ungreased baking sheet and bake 10 to 15 minutes in a preheated 350 degree oven, stirring occasionally.

EQUIVALENT MEASUREMENTS

1 tablespoon	=	3 teaspoons
⅛ cup (1 fluid ounce)	=	2 tablespoons
¼ cup (2 fluid ounces)	=	4 tablespoons
⅓ cup	=	5⅓ tablespoons
½ cup (4 fluid ounces)	=	8 tablespoons
¾ cup (6 fluid ounces)	=	12 tablespoons
1 cup (8 fluid ounces)	=	16 tablespoons or ½ pint
2 cups (16 fluid ounces)	=	1 pint
1 quart (32 fluid ounces)	=	2 pints
½ gallon (64 fluid ounces)	=	2 quarts
1 gallon (128 fluid ounces)	=	4 quarts

HELPFUL FOOD EQUIVALENTS

½ cup butter	=	1 stick butter
1 square baking chocolate	=	1 ounce chocolate
6 ounces chocolate chips	=	1 cup chocolate chips
2¼ cups packed brown sugar	=	1 pound brown sugar
3½ cups confectioners sugar	=	1 pound confectioners sugar
2 cups granulated sugar	=	1 pound granulated sugar
4 cups all-purpose flour	=	1 pound all-purpose flour
1 cup grated cheese	=	4 ounces cheese
3 cups sliced carrots	=	1 pound carrots
½ cup sliced celery	=	1 rib celery
½ cup chopped onion	=	1 medium onion
1 cup chopped green pepper	=	1 large green pepper

GENERAL INSTRUCTIONS

TRANSFERRING PATTERNS

When entire pattern is shown, place a piece of tracing paper over pattern and trace pattern, marking all placement symbols and markings. Cut out traced pattern.

When one-half of pattern is shown, fold tracing paper in half and place fold along dashed line of pattern. Trace pattern half, marking all placement symbols and markings; turn folded paper over and draw over all markings. Cut out traced pattern; unfold pattern and lay it flat.

SEWING SHAPES

1. Center pattern on wrong side of 1 fabric piece and use fabric marking pencil to draw around pattern. DO NOT CUT OUT SHAPE.
2. Place fabric pieces right sides together. Leaving an opening for turning, carefully sew pieces together directly on pencil line.
3. Leaving a ¼" seam allowance, cut out shape. Clip seam allowance at curves and corners. Turn shape right side out. Use the rounded end of a small crochet hook to completely turn small areas.

MAKING PADDED SHAPES

1. Use cardboard shape as a pattern and cut 1 shape from batting. Use fabric marking pencil to draw around pattern on wrong side of fabric. Cut out fabric shape ½" larger than drawn line.
2. Center batting then cardboard on wrong side of fabric shape. At ½" intervals, clip edge of fabric shape to ⅛" from edge of cardboard. Pulling fabric taut, glue cut edges of fabric to top (wrong side) of cardboard.

HOW TO STENCIL

1. Trace pattern onto tracing paper. Use transfer paper to transfer design to center of tagboard. Place tagboard on cutting mat or a thick layer of newspapers. Use craft knife to cut out stencil.
2. (*Note:* Use removable tape to mask any cutout areas on stencil next to area being painted.) Hold or tape stencil in place. Use a clean, dry stencil brush for each color of paint. Dip brush in paint and remove excess paint on a paper towel. Brush should be almost dry to produce good results. Beginning at edge of cutout area, apply paint in a stamping motion. If desired, shade design by stamping additional paint around edge of cutout area. Carefully remove stencil and allow paint to dry.

JAR LID FINISHING

1. For jar lid insert, use flat part of a jar lid (same size as jar lid used in storing food) as a pattern and cut 1 circle each from cardboard, batting, and fabric. Matching edges, glue batting to cardboard. Center fabric circle right side up on batting; glue edge of fabric to batting.
2. Just before presenting gift, remove screw ring from filled jar, being careful not to break seal of lid. Place jar lid insert in screw ring and screw in place over lid. If food was canned using the water-bath method and seal of lid is broken, jar must be refrigerated.

FABRIC BAG

1. To determine width of fabric needed, add ½" to finished width of bag; to determine length of fabric needed, double the finished height of bag and add 1½". Cut fabric the determined width and length.
2. With right sides together and matching short edges, fold fabric in half; finger press folded edge (bottom of bag). Using a ¼" seam allowance and thread to match fabric, sew sides of bag together.
3. Press top edge of bag ¼" to wrong side; press ½" to wrong side again and stitch in place.
4. For bag with a flat bottom, match each side seam to fold line at bottom of bag; sew across each corner 1" from point (Fig. 1). Turn bag right side out.

Fig. 1

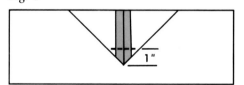

GIFT BOX 1

Note: Use this technique to cover square or rectangular cardboard boxes that are already assembled, such as shoe boxes, department store gift boxes, or some candy boxes.

1. For box lid, refer to Fig. 1 to measure length and width of lid (including sides). Add $1\frac{1}{2}''$ to each measurement; cut wrapping paper the determined size.

Fig. 1

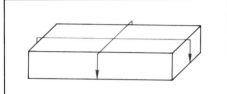

2. Place wrapping paper right side down on a flat surface; center box lid, top side down, on paper. For 1 short side of box lid, cut paper diagonally from corners to within $\frac{1}{16}''$ of lid (Fig. 2). Fold short edge of paper up and over side of lid (Fig. 3); crease paper along folds and tape edge in place inside lid. Repeat for remaining short side.

Fig. 2

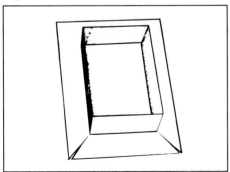

Fig. 3

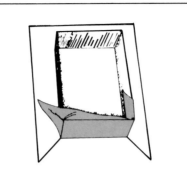

3. For 1 long side of box lid, fold paper as shown in Fig. 4; crease paper along folds. Fold paper up and over side of lid; crease paper along folds and tape edge in place inside lid. Repeat for remaining long side.

Fig. 4

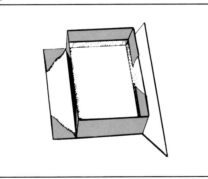

4. Repeat Steps 1 - 3 for bottom of box.

GIFT BOX 2

Note: Use this technique to cover cardboard boxes that are unassembled or are easily unfolded, such as cake or pie boxes.

1. Unfold box to be covered. Cut a piece of wrapping paper $1''$ larger on all sides than unfolded box. Place wrapping paper right side down on a flat surface.
2. For a small box, apply spray adhesive to outside of entire box. Place box, adhesive side down, on paper; press firmly to secure.
3. For a large box, apply spray adhesive to bottom of box. Center box, adhesive side down, on paper; press firmly to secure. Applying spray adhesive to 1 section at a time, repeat to secure remaining sections of box to paper.
4. Use a craft knife to cut paper even with edges of box. If box has slits, use craft knife to cut through slits from inside of box.
5. Reassemble box.

Continued on page 124

GENERAL INSTRUCTIONS (continued)

CROSS STITCH

COUNTED CROSS STITCH

Work 1 Cross Stitch to correspond to each colored square on the chart. For horizontal rows, work stitches in 2 journeys (Fig. 1). For vertical rows, complete each stitch as shown in Fig. 2. When working over 2 fabric threads, work Cross Stitch as shown in Fig. 3. When the chart shows a Backstitch crossing a colored square (Fig. 4), a Cross Stitch (Fig. 1, 2, or 3) should be worked first; then the Backstitch (Fig. 8) should be worked on top of the Cross Stitch.

Fig. 3

Fig. 4

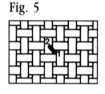

HALF CROSS STITCH (½ X)

This stitch is 1 journey of the Cross Stitch and is worked from lower left to upper right. Fig. 7 shows the Half Cross Stitch worked over 2 fabric threads.

Fig. 7

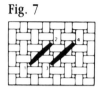

QUARTER STITCH (¼ X)

Quarter Stitches are denoted by triangular shapes of color on the chart and on the color key. Come up at 1 (Fig. 5); then split fabric thread to go down at 2. Fig. 6 shows this technique when working over 2 fabric threads.

BACKSTITCH

For outline detail, Backstitch (shown on chart and color key by black or colored straight lines) should be worked after the design has been completed (Fig. 8).

Fig. 1

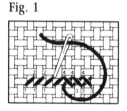

Fig. 2

Fig. 5

Fig. 6

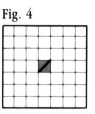

Fig. 8

CREDITS

Our sincere thank-you goes to Linda M. Perry for sharing her ideas for a book combining recipes and crafts with friendship sayings.

To Magna IV Engravers of Little Rock, Arkansas, we say thank you for the superb color reproduction and excellent pre-press preparation.

We want to especially thank photographers Mark Mathews and Ken West of Peerless Photography, Little Rock, Arkansas, for their time, patience, and excellent work.

To the talented people who helped in the creation of some of the projects and recipes in this book, we extend a special word of thanks.

My Friendship's Free, page 9: Lorraine Birmingham
Bread Cloth, page 77: Ann Townsend
Book Boxes, page 83, and *Take-out Carton,*
    page 101: Linda M. Perry

Strawberry Pie, page 21: Sandra Case
Pumpkin Butter, page 62: Carol Matthias
No-Bake Brownies, page 73: Patricia Sowers

We extend a warm thank-you to the people who assisted in making and testing the projects in this book: Mary Carlton, Barbara Hodges, Nelda Newby, and Karey Weeks.

RECIPE INDEX

Ooohs, Aaahs, & Mmms GUARANTEED!

Make this Christmas a memory they'll always cherish with *The Spirit of Christmas* from Leisure Arts. Filled with more than 160 all-new projects and recipes, this luxurious volume will lead you step-by-step through decorating your home and tree, cooking and baking for all your festive gatherings, and gift-making for everyone on your list.

- 160 Joy-filled pages
- Lavish photographs
- Easy, clear instructions

To review *The Spirit of Christmas* in your home free for 21 days, call the toll-free number on this page or write to Leisure Arts, P.O. Box 10576, Des Moines, IA 50340-0576. If you're delighted with our book, pay just $19.95 (in U.S. funds), plus postage and handling. (In Canadian funds, $26.00 plus postage and handling; a 7% goods and services tax applies to all Canadian orders.) If not completely delighted, you may return the book within 21 days and owe nothing. If you keep it, you are eligible to receive future annuals *on approval*. You are in no way obligated to buy future books, and you may cancel at any time just by notifying us. Please allow 6-8 weeks for delivery. Limited time offer.

Also available at your local needlecraft shop!

FREE FOR 21 DAYS
CALL TOLL FREE 1-800-666-6326